Feed My Lambs

A Handbook for Intergenerational Cell Groups

by Lorna Jenkins

D1487159

Feed My Lambs
A Handbook for Intergenerational Cell Groups

Copyright © 1995, by Lorna Jenkins

Published by TOUCH Ministries International Pte Ltd
66/68 East Coast Road
#06-00 GRTH Building
Singapore 1542
Tel: 65-440-8821   Fax: 65-440-5205

Cover and page layout design by Eric How
Illustrations by Benji Chan

ISBN 981-00-6318-0

Available from:
TOUCH Resource Pte Ltd
3 Marine Parade Central
Singapore 1544
Tel: 65-440-7544   Fax: 65-440-4586

TOUCH Outreach Ministries, Inc.
P.O. Box 19888
Houston. TX 77079
U.S.A.
Tel: 1-800-735-5865   Fax: 713-497-0904

TOUCH International (SA)
P.O. Box 1223
Newcastle 2940
South Africa
Tel: (3431) 28111   Fax: (3431) 24211

Printed by BAC Printers
Singapore

Acknowledgements

*Special thanks to Geraldine Woo, Evelyn Cheok, Camille Burner
and all the Children's Ministry Staff of Faith Community Baptist Church*

Foreword

The Sunday School movement began in warehouses to teach Christianity to London's street waifs. In Spurgeon's day, it was insulting to suggest Christian parents should send their children to a Sunday School. In previous generations, Christian parents felt responsible for the spiritual nurture of their children. Gradually, the movement penetrated the churches.

Parents relinquished their responsibility for the spiritual development of their children, sending them instead to the church Sunday School. Soon, lesson materials became a profitable industry. Denominations saw the dollar profit in further developing the system, and seminaries introduced new courses for "Religious Education Directors." Churches spent massive sums building annexes for Sunday School classes, used for only an hour a week.

How Satan must have laughed with glee! He had fragmented the family by convincing the people of God to release to strangers the task of developing Christian values in their children. Nothing could have been more distant from God's intention than that children be instructed by their parents.

Liturgical churches added a pastor's catechism class for children, leading to church membership. Little emphasis was placed on the child forming a personal relationship with Jesus Christ. Among the evangelicals, parents began to shop for the church that would best meet the needs of their children, often shifting from one church to another for no better reason than to give their children a better "program" on Sundays.

In the Cell Church, the paradigm shift requires a rethinking of what should happen to our children. Thus, the Intergenerational Cell Groups have been developing in this movement. Intergenerational Cell Groups are built on the Biblical principles of returning to the parents and the Basic Christian Communities (Cells) the responsibility for the spiritual development of the children.

No other phase of transition from traditional church life is more difficult than to abandon Sunday School for children. For over 100 years, we have trained parents to assign to the organized church the spiritual care of their children. The retraining must begin with adults, and must extend to the last infant in our Cell Groups.

Lorna Jenkins has been prepared by the Father to lead us all into this transition. This book is the result of years of study and relating to children and their parents. F aith Community Baptist Church of Singapore is the model she uses to illustrate the structures described in this book. Their commitment to the shift is solid, even though it is in the beginning stages.

A few nights ago, I was praying with others for Lawrence Khong, the Senior Pastor, just before he entered the pulpit to preach. Four of our children saw us and came directly to join us. As they lifted their hands to pray for our pastor along with us, I realized that they have already caught the truth that, as Christians, they are also ministers. May God guide you to join us in this paradigm shift!

Dr. Ralph W. Neighbour, Jr.

To my husband, Brian, who has borne
my comings and goings and
has still encouraged me to pursue the call of God.

Contents

Appendixes

Introduction

When the cell group church came into being, many people tried to continue Sunday School the way it had always been. However the Spirit of God began to stir up a concern in the hearts of parents and leaders: If cell groups are good for adults, shouldn't they also be a blessing to children? So churches began to convert Sunday School into cell groups and this worked with varying success.

Some parents wanted to bring their children to their cell groups with them so that the whole family could experience their Christian lives together. This was tried experimentally in a number of churches around the world and many families found new joy as parents and children worshiped and ministered together.

I, too, found this a highly desirable way of integrating the family into the cell group church. Over the last year, however, God has been expanding my vision. It was never His plan for the family to be fragmented within the life of the church. The church should be a supportive spiritual family to surround the natural family, but it should not replace the family as the spiritual guide for the children.

As the Lord brings this age to a close, He plans to do a new thing in His church. No longer is the family to be broken up by our structures. He intends to turn the hearts of the fathers to their children and the hearts of the children to their parents (Malachi 4:6). If this does not happen, God declares that He will strike the land with a curse.

Today, God is raising up people with a new sensitivity of His heart towards children. He is calling families to come together again, in worship, ministry and service. Children need to experience the Christian life with their parents, and parents need to include their children in their Christian walk.

Intergenerational Cell Groups are a way of doing what God wants in the church today. Let's be bold enough to follow God's plan so that He can truly bless our families.

I pray for you as you take the first steps.

Lorna Jenkins

The Unwelcome Child

Child: May I come to your cell today
To see you worship, sing and pray?

Adult: You wouldn't find it any fun.
When you are older, you may come.

Child: But I would like to come and see
And worship with the family.

Adult: The way we praise is not for you.
Go worship with the children, do.

Child: But I love Jesus, this is true!
Can't I be a disciple too?

Adult: Just wait. The time will come to pass
You'll join a New Believers' Class.

Child: May I tell you why I'm crying?
Do you know my Grandpa's dying?

Adult: When you are old enough, you'll know
That there's a time we all must go.

Child: Can you tell, I'm asking you,
Are all the Bible stories true?

Adult: Please put aside your questions, do.
If I believe it, why can't you?

Child: My friends at school say I'm a freak
Because I go to church each week.

Adult: Just take no notice what they say.
You're growing up the Christian way.

Child: Can I come in? Do I belong?
Can I do something brave or strong?

Adult: Be patient. You're the church tomorrow
When you've learned our ways to follow.

As time went by the child grew bolder
Growing taller, growing older.
Looking for love and care and nurture
Sometime … later, in the future
When someone in the church would say,
"Come! You may join our cell today."
But the child, alas, has gone away.

Lorna Jenkins

The Vision for Intergenerational Cell Groups

God loves the children and He wants them in His Kingdom. God also has a plan for them. He does leave it to us on how we choose to nurture them and lead them into mature Christian life, but He sets out clear commandments about the way we should teach them to grow spiritually. His plan has two strands:

1. Children Should Grow within a Family

Children are born into a family environment where they are loved and taught by their own parents. It is in this normal context of home life that they are nurtured, not in a school situation.

Outside his immediate family is the child's extended family of grandparents, aunts and uncles, cousins, and even family friends. Then there is the family of God – brothers and sisters in Christ so that every child has a spiritual family beyond his natural one. This spiritual family supports and encourages the natural family in leading their children in the ways of God. The natural family is not on its own.

2. Children Should Live a Full Christian Life

Nowhere does the Bible suggest that children have a second-class level of Christian life. If children have genuinely been born again they should be able to pray effectively, to worship, and to receive the Holy Spirit and His gracious gifts. They should be equipped for the spiritual attacks which surround them. They should be able to win other children and adults to Christ. They should have a heart of service and they should be good role models to their peers. In other words, God's promises are for the children as much as they are for the adults. We should not be holding the children back from what God wants to do in their lives. More often the barrier is not their immaturity but our own lack of faith.

God Makes Two Promises about Children in the Last Days:

1. He intends to turn the hearts of the fathers to their children and the hearts of the children to their fathers. (Malachi 4:6)
2. God will pour out His Spirit on the children – "Your sons and daughters will prophesy." (Joel 2:28)

God is already doing this around the world. Our churches should be open to what He is doing. We should be restoring and healing the fragments of family life broken through the structures of the church and our society. We should be releasing the children into the full life of Christ so that they can experience for themselves the reality and power of God rather than hear secondhand about His power in the past and in the lives of adults.

From around the world, I am hearing reports of what God is doing through children. Children have been caught up in revival, praying for adults and healing them. They are leading and multiplying cell groups in some countries. In one church in Central America, a 14-year-old boy is leading a cell group. He has multiplied his group five times!

God longs to bless his church through the children. He wants to bless the children and the families through the church. The church needs to provide the means to minister to whole families, and for families to minister to families. Single people are also part of families and they are important role models and leaders. Classroom seminars are not enough. Families need to live transparently, supporting and teaching one another out of their own life experience. God intends us to be a community and to retain the next generation. If the church is for adults only, the church will die!

Read It for Yourself	*Do You Agree?*
God's desire relating to children:	Churches tend to fragment families through their programs.
Deuteronomy 6:6-9; 11:18-20	
Psalms 8:2; Psalms 78:5-7	If cell groups are the church in relationship and action, the children should be there.
I Samuel 2:26; 3:19-20; 16:13	
Joel 2:28	The life of the whole family is rightfully the concern of the cell group.
Malachi 4:6	
Matthew 18:1-6; 21:15-16	
Luke 18:15-17	
Acts 21:5	

Part One

LOOKING AT THE INTERGENERATIONAL CELL GROUP

A New Testament Intergenerational Cell Group

Stephen lived in a fine three-story house. It was not his father's house. His father was a slave in the house. Dad worked for a man called Marcellus by teaching his children. Stephen's mother was a slave too. She would look after Mrs. Marcellus. Stephen was a slave because his parents were slaves. Stephen worked in the kitchens helping the cooks. Because Stephen's father was a teacher, he also used to teach Stephen during his spare time.

Sunday was a special day in the big house where Stephen lived. Stephen's master was a Christian. So were Stephen and his parents. On Sunday evening other Christians would come to the house to meet one another and to worship Jesus. Not all of them were rich people; in fact, many were quite poor. Many would bring their children. Some were slaves like Stephen. Marcellus would provide a meal for all of them. For some it was the best meal they had all week.

In those days it was not safe to be a Christian. Christians could be caught and put in prison. So the Christians devised a secret code of a special knock on the door so that Stephen's father would know it was one of them. If someone came whom he did not know, he would not ask him straight out if he were a Christian. Instead, he would draw a fish like this:

The word fish in Greek is spelled I-CH-TH-U-S-"Ichthus." In Greek, "I" is the first letter of the name "Jesus," "Ch" is the first letter of "Christ," "Th" is the first letter of God," "U" is the first letter of the word "Son," and "S" is the first letter of the word for "Savior." So the letters of the word "fish" spell out this message, "Jesus Christ, Son of God, Savior." That's why the fish sign was a code for Christians.

This was the secret code for Jesus Christ. Only Christians would recognize it. Those who did not know the sign were not Christians and they were not allowed in.

As the Christians arrived, someone would wash their feet. Sometimes it was Stephen. He would take off their sandals and wash away the dust from their feet. They always smiled and thanked him because it reminded them of how Jesus washed the feet of the disciples.

Some of them brought money and gifts to share with the others who did not have enough food and clothing. Stephen's mother would look after the gifts and later give them away. The master, Marcellus, was not the leader of the church; the leader was a tent-maker named Aquila, and his wife was Priscilla.

When they arrived, all the people would greet one another and sit down to exchange news about what had been happening to them during the week. Some would tell about being badly treated by a cruel master. Others would report about how they had been able to tell a friend about Jesus. This was a dangerous thing to do because you could be reported to the police. Some would tell of how they had to leave their homes and hide for a while because the soldiers were coming. Even the children would relate how they had avoided having to worship idols. As they told their stories the groups would praise God and thank Him that they had been able to be brave.

Then Aquila would encourage them to pray. First, they would thank God for his love and protection over them during the week; then, for the opportunity to follow Jesus even though it was dangerous. They would also pray for any of their friends who might be in prison, especially their friend Paul who was in prison in Rome.

They would pray for the sick people in their group. They would lay their hands on them and place a few drops of oil on their heads. Sometimes they were even healed right there. They would pray for people with problems, especially for those slaves who had cruel masters.

After a while, the group would begin to worship God. They would sing songs, some of which were from the Bible and some written by other Christians. People would also share stories they had heard about the things Jesus used to do when He was alive. They did not have the New Testament to read.

Some of the people would speak in a special language which no one could understand and then someone else would interpret for the group what had been said. Sometimes someone would speak a special message from God to help and encourage the people. Stephen liked hearing the stories about Jesus. It made Jesus seem real, as though He Himself had been there. Sometimes Stephen would feel God saying something in his heart and then he would tell the others what it was. Then Aquila would pick up a loaf of bread from the meal table, and he would thank God for it and remember how Jesus died for them all. Then he would break it and share it around the group so everyone would have a piece. When Stephen took the piece of bread and ate it, tears would sometimes come into his eyes as he thought about Jesus being nailed to the cross. He had seen people being nailed to a cross and it was horrible.

They would eat the rest of their meal together while enjoying talking to their friends. When everyone had finished eating, Aquila would take a cup full of wine and ask God to bless it. He would pass it around the group for everyone to have a sip. Stephen knew that the wine reminded them of the blood of Jesus which takes away the sin of the world. He was glad that he had decided to choose Jesus as his God and Lord.

After the meal they would sit and talk a bit longer and sometimes there would be a letter from their friend, Paul, who was in prison. Usually Priscilla would read it out because she was a good reader. When they heard the letter, the people often wanted to talk about it, but by this time Stephen would be getting sleepy, so his mother would tell him he could go to bed. One by one the people would slip out of the house but not all together because they did not want to attract attention.

Talking It Over

That's how people used to go to church when Stephen was alive.
What do you think are some of the good things about it?
What are some of the things you wouldn't like?

*W*HAT IS AN INTERGENERATIONAL CELL GROUP?

When Keith's group decided to become an Intergenerational Cell Group, some of the group members felt very threatened because they didn't know what it would be like. "Will the children be with us all the time?" asked Matthew. "How can we talk about personal things when the children are there?"
"Suppose the children misbehave and we have to keep interrupting the group to deal with them?" asked Paul.
"My baby needs to be fed at 10 pm. What if the group hasn't finished?" Lynne's baby was only four weeks old.

An Intergenerational Cell Group is a cell group that welcomes children as full members. It does not set up any age barriers. Although the children may have a separate subgroup during the evening, they belong to the whole cell group and they can bless and minister to the adults as well as be blessed by the adults. Such cell groups include the children in all their activities: prayer, praise, spiritual growth and evangelism. Families and singles mix together to form a wider family of Christ.

Everyone has important questions to ask about Intergenerational Cell Groups. This book will give you some guidelines but it can't cover every possible question because every group is different. Some groups will have very few children and others will have two children for every adult! Some of the children will be very young and some of them will be pre-teens. Each Intergenerational Cell Group will need to ask God for solutions to its problems.

Don't give up when you hit the first problem. Relationships always bring problems because we are problem people! Satan loves to tell us that Intergenerational Cell Groups will not work. He does not want them to work because he knows that the spiritual family is powerful in the lives of the children.

The children will have problems too. They may not want to belong to a group where there are adults. They have learned that when adults get together, things get boring. They have to sit still and listen. When children discover that the cell group respects them and wants them to participate in all that is happening, they rapidly change their minds. One child who was in a new Intergenerational Cell Group did not want to go home!

How Old Should Children Be to Join an Intergenerational Cell Group?

Most mothers hesitate about bringing their little ones. They are afraid that the babies will interrupt and disturb the others in the group. If they have to remove the child from the group all the time, they might as well not go. If the group is truly intergenerational, the babies and toddlers belong there. A child is part of the spiritual family at birth, not when he/she is four. Babies and toddlers will respond in different ways. You can plan for babies to sleep through the group and you may feed them at the right time. Some toddlers will fall asleep if the group gets late.

However, many toddlers like to be in the action and they find it hard to sit still. Do they really need to? They can praise and worship or they can wander around the group without causing disturbance. Intergenerational groups need to be flexible and tolerant.

Will the Older Children Want to Join the Group?

If there is only one older child in the group, he/she may wish to stay with the adults. However, if you give older children some responsibility and make them leaders of the younger children, they usually join in with the subgroup quite happily.

Should Teenagers Be Part of the Intergenerational Cell Group?

In many cell group churches, the Youth Department has cell groups for teenagers. At their stage of life, they like to feel a little independent from their parents and could be reluctant to share openly if their parents are present. However, if they have been part of an Intergenerational Cell Group when they were younger they may like to continue with it.

How Long Should the Children and the Adults Be Together?

This time may be fairly flexible and it could change from session to session. The children usually participate in the icebreaker, the praise and worship, the news and prayer and also family time. (See page 29) Then they go off to their own group for their edification, sharing and activity time. Later, the two groups come together to report what they had been doing.

Children have a different life experience from adults, so they talk about different things. They need to be part of a spiritual family but they also need to talk as children, just as we need to talk as adults. Also, time should be allowed for some physical activity. They can't sit still for too long. The adults need to make concessions for them. Children should not be asked to stay in the Kids' Slot (the children's subgroup) for too long.

When and Where Should the Cell Group Meet?

The cell group will need to meet on a day when the children do not have to get up early the next morning. Cell meetings should not continue to midnight. Families need to get their children home even if some people want to stay longer. Some groups meet earlier in the evening, even over a pot-luck meal. Working people come directly to the cell group. Some groups prefer to meet at weekends.

You will probably need to choose a home which is large enough for the children to meet in a separate area. Two adjoining apartments would work well. It just takes a bit of creativity. Children can meet in a kitchen, a hallway, a yard, a bedroom (with the beds pushed back), in a garage, or even in the open area beneath their apartment.

Multiplying Intergenerational Cell Groups

When it comes time to multiply an Intergenerational Cell Group, it has to be done on a slightly different basis. It will not be entirely based on adult numbers; the ratio of children to adults and the number of children in the respective families will have to be taken into consideration. It would be ideal to have at least one family in each new cell group so that both groups could operate intergenerationally. However, it may not be easy to separate children from people in the cell group to whom they have become deeply attached.

Multiplication may come a little sooner if the number of children in the cell group gets too large. In other groups the multiplication may be delayed a little so that there can be children in both cell groups. The children who are going to be with the new leader need an opportunity to get to know him/her before the multiplication takes place. They need to learn to like and trust the leader.

Leadership of the Kids' Slot

The children's subgroup (the Kids' Slot) is usually led by one of the group members, who take turns to be with the children. In this way the children get to know several of the adults. However the children will "own" all the members of the cell group. They will say, "That's Mr Lee. He belongs to *my* cell group..."

Not every member of the cell group will feel able to lead the children. That does not mean they should keep aloof. Sometimes they can visit the children in their Kids' Slot and let the children talk to them. They may talk to the children or play with them at a social event, or they may decide to pray specially for a child. Many people are amazed to discover they can form a friendship with a child.

The Intergenerational Cell Group is for everyone. The children are not there as visitors or as less important members. When something is being planned, their needs should be considered too.

$\mathscr{I}$NTERGENERATIONAL CELL GROUPS BLESS PEOPLE

God desires to bless his church through the children. They are not a hindrance or a burden in the life of the church or in the life of the cell group. People are afraid the children will spoil the cell group meeting because they have been taught to believe that children are disruptive and they cannot worship or talk seriously. Many parents secretly fear their children will expose some of the weaknesses of their home life. Other parents worry that their children will be bored in the cell group.

Intergenerational Cell Groups Can Be Encouraging for Everyone
As long as we listen to the fears which Satan plants in us, we cannot hear what God is saying to us. God wants to bless families as we share our joys and hurts and worries. All families have their ups and downs. All parents and children have some in-house battles. When we struggle alone, both parents and children feel that no one in the world understands. In a cell group we learn from, and pray for one another. Families can become friends.

Read this Testimony:
"Some years ago my family was involved in a small group where our children had a recognized place and function. About 10 families met in a large home on Friday evenings. We sang, told stories and shared family secrets. Then the children went off and did what they wanted. The adults participated in prayer and discussion. We concluded with supper. We formed relationships which still continue today. The most recent gathering was a birthday party for myself and the wedding of one of the daughters."

In Intergenerational Cell Groups, Children See for Themselves
In the normal course of life, few children get to see their parents living out their Christian lives. Daddy goes off to work in the morning and comes home, tired at night. Children can be amazed to see Dad leading worship or praying for someone's needs. They may be just as surprised to learn that Mommy has been talking about Jesus to a friend in the same apartment block.

Children also need to know that God is working in the lives of other people, too. There may be grandparents who can tell stories of how God has led them through life. Single people are specially important. Children like single people because they are not parents. Children listen to single people and copy them.

We don't have to be perfect to be good models for children. Children need to know that Christians struggle and do wrong at times. However, God is working within each one of us. This encourages the children who often feel that they alone are always wrong and therefore are never acceptable to grown-ups or to God.

In Intergenerational Cell Groups, Children Grow Spiritually

When children discover they are respected in a cell group, participation becomes natural. I've seen a child as young as four hurry across the room to lay hands on a person who is sick. They learn to worship and even to lead the adults in worship. They will tell you about their own prayer needs and pray for the needs of others. They can begin to hear the word of the Lord and to share it with others. They may even use a prayer language. In a cell group it is safe for children to ask their awkward questions. If the parents do not have the answers, someone else in the group will know or they will find out the answers.

As the children begin to follow Jesus, they will probably want to remember His love in the Lord's Supper. In the family context of the cell group, the members will know of the child's faith and will be able to help him/her understand when the right time comes. Children who wish to be baptized will also have the support and discernment of their cell group.

God Wants to Bless the Events of Family Life

Every family has special events, some of them wonderful and some of them sad. God is a part of all these and in the Intergenerational Cell Group we are able to celebrate or sympathize, expressing the heart of God to the family. The cell group journeys through all the milestones of the children's lives, their successes and their disappointments. Out of the shared life experience comes a relational bond. Children know they belong within their Christian community.

Children Can Even Share in Outreach!

When new families enter the cell group, the children can help in making them feel at home. Adults can help children invite their friends to cell group events. They can also get to know their friends' parents.

A cell group may develop an interest group involving children. During school vacation, for example, they may run a neighborhood club in which both adults and children are involved. Or, they may sponsor a community service group to unchurched children.

"We're new to the church. Where do we fit in?"

Children can be involved in cell group evangelistic outreaches. In one church, a 10-year-old boy was on a visitation team in the community. As the group was mowing the grass for a man in his home, the boy felt God's prompting to pray for this man. The team leader asked the man if the boy could pray for him, and when he did, God broke down the hard barriers and the man wept out the tragedy which had overtaken him.* Children can be very sensitive to the needs of others.

When the cell group runs special harvest events, the children can reach out to the families of the people who are invited. When children have won a friend to Christ they will never be the same.

These Things Take Time

All these blessings will not come in the first week. An Intergenerational Cell Group takes time to be a community with everyone learning as they go along. Mistakes are inevitable, so both adults and children will need to be patient and forgiving just as Jesus is.

*Steven Sjogren, "Children are Natural Soul-winners," Charisma Magazine March 1994

*P*ROGRAM FOR AN INTERGENERATIONAL CELL GROUP

Children and Adults Together
Welcome and Icebreaker
Worship and praise
Reporting news
Family Time
Prayer (including the children)
The Lord's Supper or any other special event (Could also come at the end.)

Children and Adults Separate

Adults
Edification
Prayer and Ministry
Planning events
Sharing the Vision (Prayer for non believers)

Kids' Slot
Edification: Talking about Sunday message
Review Scripture memory verse
Support Activity
Share the Vision
Praying for unbelieving friends and family
Praying for the world
Planning for service to others

Children Return to Adult Group
Report significant happenings
Prayer
Food and Blessing

These items can be moved around or even omitted according to the needs of the group that week. It is not a fixed structure.

$\mathcal{W}$HO CONTROLS THE INTERGENERATIONAL CELL GROUP?

Who is in charge of an Intergenerational Cell Group?
Suppose people cannot agree about the children's behavior?
Can the hosts make any rules about their house?
What do we do if people behave badly?
What is a Group Agreement like?

In an Intergenerational Cell Group there is only one leader and he is appointed by the church. This does not mean he has to do everything for the children, but ultimately he is responsible for the whole group. The leader is the shepherd and is concerned for the spiritual well-being of everyone in the group.

However, the parents of the children also have a special place. They have a God-given authority over their own children and the cell group members should support them and build them up in that authority. The hosts of the home where the cell group is being held also have some authority over the way people behave in their home. The leaders who are with the children during the Kids' Slot have delegated authority during the time when the children are under their care.

Conflict of Authority

Sometimes tensions can build up between these people or among the cell group members. Often this arises because different families have different standards of discipline for their children. What is permissible for one child is forbidden for another. Other people whose children are grown up are often shocked at the standards of behavior among modern children.

The Group Agreement

Many of these concerns can be anticipated and prevented if the cell group, both children and adults, understand the expectations of the group from the start. It is always better to negotiate before a crisis arises. A Group Agreement helps the group to consider the possibilities and to set down guidelines for everyone to follow.

Some people find a Group Agreement too legalistic a way of handling the situation but that depends on how it is viewed. It would be wrong if the Group Agreement is viewed as a business contract. However, the cell group is family and every family has some understanding about what is acceptable and what is not.

A Covenant

The Group Agreement is more like a covenant. The cell group meeting has to be pleasant and useful and the needs of others have to be considered. When the Group Agreement is written the children are allowed to make suggestions. They pray over it and ask the Lord's help to keep faith with one another. Then everyone signs the Agreement to show they have accepted their responsibilities (See sample on page 33).

House Rules

Cell group members must bear in mind that they are invited guests in the homes where the meetings are held. So it is only courteous to behave in the way the hosts would wish, even if the guests have different rules in their own homes.

If a cell group is meeting regularly in the same home, the house rules should be set by the host family. If the cell group is moving from house to house, the group should work out the house rules together (See sample on page 37).

When Trouble Arises

Every so often, even in the best cell groups "accidents" will occur. Perhaps an object gets broken or is accidentally damaged. Or, parents may allow their children to misbehave far beyond the tolerance level of the cell group. Arguments may take place either between parents and children or even among the adults.

When these happen, the Cell Group Leader, the authority under Christ, will talk to the people involved and help them see what their Christian response should be. God will give him wisdom to lead in this matter and the Holy Spirit will bring a word from the Bible into his mind. If it is appropriate, the whole matter may be discussed in the cell group and prayed over together. The children can pray also, especially if they are involved.

Likewise, when people behave harshly or wrongly the Cell Group Leader should try to encourage reconciliation, repentance and forgiveness, whether between an adult and a child, or between the adults. Children need to know that adults can behave badly at times and that Christians know how to say they are sorry. If the Cell Group Leader cannot handle the matter, he should call on the Zone Supervisor or the Pastor for help.

Minor Misbehavior

If occasionally the children behave badly, their parents have the first responsibility to correct them. If the parents ignore the behavior, the Cell Group Leader would tactfully remind them of the Group Agreement. Problems often arise when food is served, because children often want to be served first. They can be greedy or they may spill food on the floor. Children need to be taught how to eat food politely in public and in someone else's home.

If the parents are absent when the children break the rules, any cell group member can check them gently, but they should not punish them. During the Kids' Slot, the leader rostered has authority to control the children. The best control comes through love and respect.

GROUP AGREEMENT FOR
_____CELL GROUP

Date:_____

Every member in this cell group, both adults and children, want to care for each other. We want to grow in our Christian lives and to be a part of God's big family.
Our names are:

_____

_____

_____

_____

_____

_____

_____

_____

_____

_____

The adults will welcome the children and try to be their friends. The children will respect the adults and be friendly to them too.

Our Cell Group Leader is _____
He/she looks after the whole group. We will obey him/her.

Other cell group members will take turns leading the children.

The Children's Coordinator is _____

Our Family Reporter, _____,
looks after birthdays and other events.

Time Together

Sometimes the whole group will want to be together. This will be for worship, news reporting, prayer, food, icebreakers, and any other activities. The adults will do their best to involve the children and make them feel part of it. The children will try to cooperate with the adults and take part in all the activities. Sometimes the group will talk about family events and they will pray for one another.

Kids' Slot

Sometimes the adults will want to talk about things on their own and the children will want to do the same. When the Cell Group Leader gives the word, the children and one of the adults, will go to another location to continue the cell meeting on their own. Later the two groups will report to each other about what they did.

How We are Going to Behave in Our Cell Group

For Everyone

Because we love and respect each other:

- We will be polite to one another, regardless of age.
- We will not say unkind things about anyone else in the group.
- We will learn to accommodate one another.
- We will listen to one another. We will try to find answers to problems and not just criticize or stay away.
- We will remember that Jesus is with us and we will behave in a way to please him.

Because we are God's family:

- We will pray for one another by name and will keep a prayer card to remember everyone by name.
- We will attend cell group as often as we can. We will not let other things keep us away.

Because we trust one another:

- We will tell each other about things that go wrong in our lives.
- We will not talk to others about things we hear in the cell group.
- We will remind one another of the promise and commitment we have made to the group.

Memo for the Children

We will remember that some adults are sensitive to noisy games, so we will be considerate by not shouting or running around inside the house.

During worship time we will try to worship God and not distract the others.

We will not talk about our parents or family to the whole group, unless we have permission.

We will remember that God wants us to obey our parents and the Cell Group Leader.

We will obey the House Rules set by the host family.

In our own Kids' Slot, we will work together with children of all ages, and we will not fight with one another. We will respect the person leading the Kids' Slot.

We will talk to adults politely remembering they deserve our respect. We will try to be their friends.

When food is offered, we will try to serve others before ourselves.

Other things you would like to add:

_____

_____

_____

_____

_____

_____

Memo for the Adults

We expect parents to take the final responsibility for their own children, but we will help and support them.

We will be patient with the children even when we find them difficult to handle. We will talk to them, help them and try to understand why they responded in the way they did.

If a child's parents are not members of the group one of the members of the group will act as an adopted aunt or uncle.

We will support the House Rules set by the host family and any adult may check a child who is breaking them.

Parents will not talk about their children to the whole group unless the child has given them permission to do so.

Parents may delegate their authority to check their children to another person if that is appropriate and they should tell their children when they do so.

The Cell Group Leader will not ignore the children or keep them sitting for too long without involving them in the group activity. We will not keep the meeting going too late so as not to bore or tire the children. If we wish to talk further we will arrange another time or allow the parents to take their children home.

Other things you would like to add:

_____

_____

_____

_____

$\mathscr{A}$N EXAMPLE OF HOUSE RULES

1.   It is not good to run inside the house.

2.   It is not good to put one's feet or jump on the furniture.

3.   Most people do not like their guests to turn on the television, stereo or computer without their permission. Seek consent before playing any musical instruments.

4.   It is not polite for a guest to go into the bedrooms or the kitchen unless invited.

5.   It is not good to play with objects or toys without the permission of the host. It is embarrassing if something gets broken. Writing on walls and furniture is not allowed.

6.   It is polite to help to tidy up any mess before leaving.

7.   It is polite to ask the host first before using the bathroom.

8.   It is not polite to eat or drink until invited to do so. It is kind to first offer food to someone else before you start eating.

9.   Children and adults should thank the hosts for their kindness and should say "Goodbye" politely.

Not to be broken

Part Two

The People of the Intergenerational Cell Group

*W*HO'S WHO IN AN INTERGENERATIONAL CELL GROUP?

The Cell Group Leader

The Cell Group Leader leads the whole group, the children as well as the adults. He/she is in control of the overall working of the group.

This does not mean that the Leader does everything. The Leader can delegate responsibility to other cell members in different areas of the cell group life. The Children's Coordinator will inform the Leader of what is happening with the children. If a problem arises, the cell members do not try to solve it alone but they talk it over with the Cell Group Leader. If the problem cannot be solved, the Cell Group Leader asks the IGC Facilitator for help.

The Hosts

The people who invite the cell group to their homes deserve special consideration. They usually make special preparations for the cell group. When there are children, they need to prepare two locations for the two subgroups. Parents should teach their children to respect the hosts' home and to obey the House Rules.

The Children's Coordinator

This person is the team leader for the adult children's helpers. Suppose six people in the cell group are prepared to take turns leading the Kids' Slot for the children. One of them needs to be the Coordinator. He/she will arrange the roster, remind helpers of their turn each week, and distribute to the helpers the material supplied by the Children's Ministry.

The Children's Coordinator will prepare a monthly report for the Children's Ministry; this can be a simple postcard which includes the names of the children who attended, some things that happened, perhaps an answered prayer or a special need. If a child makes a spiritual decision or is facing a crisis, the Children's Ministry staff would like to know so they can help the parents and the cell group.

The Children's Coordinator is not totally responsible for the children and should not be with the children all the time. He/she is merely an organizer. Everyone in the cell group shares responsibility for the children.

Children's Helpers

These are the cheerful volunteers who take turns each week to lead the Kids' Slot. Without them, Intergenerational Cell Groups would not be possible. Not all cell group members are automatically rostered to take turns leading the Kids' Slot. It is a calling, not a chore. People who do this should be ready to find some wonderful friends among the children and to have some good times with them.

It does not matter that the children do not have the same leader each week. The children learn to identify with all the adults in the cell group so they will accept the leader rostered for the day. Even the people who are not regularly on the roster should visit the Kids' Slot occasionally to get to know the children. One older university professor found to his surprise that the children loved him.

If there are older children in the group, they can be official junior leaders in the Kids' Slot. They enjoy responsibility and are often very caring towards the younger children. Teens also do an excellent job. Senior Citizens can make good grandparents to the children.

The Family Reporter

This person has the responsibility of keeping in touch with what is going on in the lives of the cell group families. Do not limit it to just birthdays; it should include job changes, promotions, exams, sports achievements, new school classes, visits overseas, births, baptisms or any other event in the lives of the families.

Each week the Family Reporter will have the opportunity to share family news and talk with the person/s involved. It is a time for prayer and blessing. This is especially important for children who do not have parents in the group.

Parents

God has given parents authority over their children. However when they are in the cell group, they also acknowledge the authority of the Cell Group Leader, because he/she is overseeing the whole group. The Cell Group Leader will encourage parents to allow their children maximum participation in the cell group.

Many parents are uncomfortable with Intergenerational Cell Groups because they fear their children will embarrass them and many parents are easily embarrassed. They are sensitive to minor restlessness and disturbance which may not upset anyone else in the group. One mother recently refused to bring her child, because the child kept talking quietly during the prayer time. She would take no notice of the protests of the group that the child was not disturbing anyone.

Parents feel this way because they are afraid the group will criticize them or think they are bad parents. The group should keep on reassuring them. God is not displeased with the happy murmuring of a child. Often such parents desperately need the relief of another person who can confidently handle their child. Other parents with older children can help nervous young parents.

The Singles

Singles should be patient. They may be parents themselves one day! Children need many adult friends, not just parents. God calls the whole cell group to be spiritual family to the children. Because singles are not emotionally involved with the children, often they can relax with them and enjoy them more. They do not have to deal with them day after day, so children may be a new experience for them.

Singles make very good children's helpers because they can be very creative in trying out new ideas. Parents tend to get stereotyped because they haven't time to be anything else.

Children often relate to singles in a special way. They look up to them as "heroes". To the children, singles are more like themselves even though they are grown up. Singles may still be living at home with their parents and that means they do not count as "parent figures". They do not have the authority that comes from dealing with matters of discipline so the children will be more relaxed in their presence. At the same time the singles should expect respect from the children. It's a privilege to be an "Aunt" or "Uncle" to a child.

The Children

It's often hard for adults to recognize children as full members of the group. The children feel they are on-lookers or appendages to their parents. It takes time to recognize the children as real people and to learn to appreciate their natural and spiritual gifts.

It's also hard for the children. Many children have never had to associate with adults before, apart from their parents and relatives. They do not know what to do; so they often do the wrong things, or they show off.

Sometimes, they do not even know they are doing anything wrong. They need experience more than scolding. The group should help the children find their place within it and not criticize them for their mistakes. If the children are made to feel they have been bad or stupid, they will not want to come.

The IGC Facilitator

If you are a small and growing church, you will probably need only one IGC Facilitator. This could be your children's pastor or deacon. In a larger church where you have many Intergenerational Cell Groups you will probably need several facilitators. These are people who help and train the Children's Coordinators. An IGC Facilitator can really handle only about five IGCs. This means attending from time to time, keeping in touch with the leaders and acting as support and adviser if difficulties arise. The Facilitator will keep in touch with the whole group to encourage them. He/she will also report problems to the church leadership.

A NOTE TO CELL GROUP LEADERS

Dear Cell Group Leader:

When your cell group opened up to receive children, you suddenly gained some new people under your care. In one way they were always there because you cared about the families of your members. However, now you see them every week and you know them as friends.

You should not ignore the children when they are present. They have a right to be included during the time they share with the adults. Later in this book you will find some help in leading prayer and worship with the children present.

Attitudes

I know you wouldn't intentionally hurt one of these little children, but attitudes are very important. Some people cannot treat children as real people. They put on a special voice for them. They talk down to them as if they had limited intelligence. Remember: children's experience and education may be limited but their minds and their feelings are not.

Some leaders try to make the first part of the cell group just a funtime for the children. This is a mistake. The adults get sick of it very quickly and the children know it isn't the real thing. Children like to do what adults do and they like to be taken seriously.

Invite the children to help in the worship or the icebreaker or the prayer, and you will be surprised how well they do it. Give them a week to prepare. Ask the parents to help if necessary. Make sure you urge the parents to arrive on time. It would be so discouraging for children to arrive late at the cell group and find their part of the cell group meeting over.

What to Do When the Children are Present?

As soon as you are ready to begin your cell group, call the children together. They are more likely to respond to you and they should know that you are the leader of the group. They should learn to obey you. Make sure you welcome them.

Choose an icebreaker which the children can enjoy too. There are a few suggestions in the back of this book. Remember children cannot understand abstract or symbolic ideas. You need to give them clear instructions. Sometimes it can be good to pair a child with an adult for the icebreaker.

Children can worship properly if someone explains to them what is going on. They can lift their hearts to God and feel His presence. Sometimes you can use pictures to get a worship idea across. Children love to play instruments and to use their bodies to express praise. They like rhythm. Give the children time to let God speak to them. Sometimes He will show them a picture or give them a word to share with the whole group. They can learn to share a verse from their Bibles.

Sharing and Praying

When you ask the group for prayer items for the week, ask the children for their news too. Young children may take a while to share their news. Wait for them. Children can pray aloud but they may need help at first. It is a good idea to keep a prayer diary to see how God answers our prayers. Don't forget that some children may have a prayer language.

Adults can bless the children and vice versa during the cell group. Some of the more serious prayer requests of the adults might need to be held back for a time when the children are not present.

Family Events

Allow time for recognizing family events such as birthdays, births, a promotion, school exams, sickness, a new home, etc. Ask the Family Reporter to look into these things.

How Long Should the Children Be Away?

Sometimes Cell Group Leaders feel nervous about having the children with the adults, so they try to dismiss them as soon as possible. Ask God to help both the children and the adults to feel relaxed and comfortable in each other's presence.

The children should be with the adults during the icebreaker, the worship and the news-sharing time. They should be in their subgroup for about *40–60 minutes.*

They should not be allowed to run all over the house. If a problem arises in the group and the Cell Leader does not want the children back so soon, he should send a message to the Children's Helper and ask for up to half an hour longer. There should always be a game held in reserve for the children in such emergencies. If the problem is going to take longer than half an hour the Cell Leader should close the meeting and find another time to deal with the matter.

When the children return, give them time to report back to the whole group. The group should try to encourage the children. The adults should also be ready to tell of good things which have happened to them. If food is offered, help the children to learn to serve others first.

If Children Cause Trouble

It is no real answer to ask children to stay away when they misbehave. You can't help the children or the parents by isolating them. The group should pray consistently for the children and the parents.

If children do something wrong they should apologize to the person concerned. Both parents and children should learn how to deal with wrong-doing. Remind the children about the House Rules and the Agreement. Whenever children have been scolded let them also be welcomed back into the family. Do not allow them to be isolated and cut off. If they have been rebuked during the cell group their parents should not punish them again when they get home.

A cell group is a good place to model forgiveness and restoration. Many families do not practice forgiveness in their own homes. Children do not know what it is like to be restored into a right relationship after they have been punished. If adults act badly towards children they should ask for forgiveness.

Many parents feel ashamed when their child misbehaves. The cell group should support parents at these times. All children misbehave at one time or another and it is no time to condemn the parents. Instead, offer ministry, practical help and encouragement. The group might like to get some help on parenting so that they can learn together.

Pastoring the Children (See page 113)

Children can be so cute or bouncy or quiet or noisy, that we forget that they also have pastoral needs. Often the children do not know that they can share their problems with someone who can help them. Sometimes children do not understand their parent's actions and they feel unloved. Remember that in family relationships the children often blame themselves for being in the wrong.

It's hard for the Cell Group Leader to minister to all the children and adults in the group. If you recognize that a child has a problem and you do not know what to do about it, ask for help. You could talk to the parents, a Children's Ministry Leader, or a Zone Pastor.

In your regular routine, show an interest in the children. Make sure you speak to the children individually. You can talk to them when you phone the home. If a child is sick or has achieved something, a special phonecall is very important. At social events, spend a little time playing with them. It is a good investment to win their respect so they will cooperate with you in the future.

You will never know how dynamic and exciting your cell group can be until you take the risk of including children. They will transform your worship, your prayer and your relationships. They will bring some problems but none of them are insurmountable. You will learn to thank God for the children in your cell group.

Checklist for Cell Group Leaders

❑ Do I know the names of the children in my group and to which families they belong?

❑ Do the parents and children know how an Intergenerational Cell Group works?

❑ Have I talked with the host families about the House Rules they want to enforce?

❑ Have I talked with the Children's Coordinator about how long the Kids' Slot should be? Is there a game which the children can use in emergencies?

❑ Have I written to the children inviting them to become part of the Intergenerational Cell Group?

❑ Have I checked with the Family Reporter for special family events?

❑ Have I talked with the Children's Ministry Leaders about the help they can offer?

❑ Have I talked with my Zone Supervisor or Zone Pastor to let them know what we are doing and to ask for their prayers. They may like to attend one of the meetings.

❑ Have I talked to God about how nervous I feel about this change?

Lord, I've never led a cell group like this before and I'm not sure how it will work. I do know that You want the children to be part of the Kingdom and you never turn them away. So help me to love them the way You do and to be humble enough to learn, even from a child.

Amen

$\mathcal{A}$ Note to Hosts

How can you make children feel welcome and still control them?
What if the parents have different standards from yours?
Suppose damage is done to your home or possessions?
How do your own children behave towards the guests?
What should you suggest as House Rules?

Dear Hosts

How generous of you to make your home available for an Intergenerational Cell Group. You may be feeling a bit nervous because you've never had anything like this in your home before. It's not so bad having the adults but the children can be a problem. Maybe you're rather unsure about how to handle them.

I know you want to make the children feel that they are welcome in your home. This may take a bit of planning. Some children feel uncomfortable in an unfamiliar environment and sometimes they will over-compensate for their shyness by being loud and assertive. This is just a temporary stage and it should settle when they become familiar with your home and the standards of behavior you expect. Make sure you tell them what they are allowed to do and what not. The cell group should talk about the House Rules.

If you have a large home with many rooms and shelves, cupboards and expensive pieces of equipment, you can help the children by limiting the area you want them to use. Closed doors are a clear barrier. Childproof fasteners on important cupboards will limit the range of the toddlers. Safety guards on low power points are a sensible idea. Make sure that danger areas, such as swimming pools, are out of bounds to children.

Fine china ornaments or glassware should not be left within reach of small children. Older children can be taught to respect them however. If you have electronic equipment, such as stereos, or TVs which you do not wish the children to use, you can cover them with a cloth, or simply make it clear from the start that they are out of bounds. You may have some games equipment available. Tell the children if they are allowed to use it but you may want to limit the time when they can use it.

If you have a small home you may need to plan how you will cope with the additional numbers. You may arrange for the children to sit on the floor or on cushions. Sometimes even the adults are happy to be on the floor. Children should not rush in and seize the biggest chairs for themselves. Some toddlers may like a mat on the floor where they can move around without being disruptive. Some simple toys can help too.

There also needs to be a place where the children can meet separately for the **Kids' Slot.** This could be a bedroom or a balcony. They might even be able to go outside. If you use a bedroom you could push the beds together to get more floor space. Chairs are not needed. If you have good carpets you might want to cover them with an old sheet. Felt pens can make nasty marks.

Some of you may worry about coming into **conflict with the parents** of the children. When the parents allow their children to misbehave in your house, you might be too embarrassed to interfere. This is where the House Rules are important. If you can talk about your expectations before a situation develops, it is easier to raise an issue later. Think carefully about how you would want the children to behave in your home so that you can make suggestions to the parents. The Cell Group Leader should help you do this.

Of course, **accidents will happen**, even in the best of cell groups. Things can be broken or stained. I know you would not want to make a fuss about it. You should allow the cell group to decide what can be done. Together you may find a good solution. As Christians we want to care for one another. It is often good for the children to make some action of recompense within their ability.

Your own children may find it quite difficult having other children coming into their territory regularly. If they have homework or special projects they are working on, it might be wise to put them away to avoid accidents.

On the other hand, this is an opportunity to teach your children how to be hosts. Ask them how they would like to be treated if they were visiting someone else's home. Ask if there are some limits to what the visitors can touch or use.

Probably your children will need to take leadership in showing children around the house and explaining the rules, but remind them not to become "bossy" just because it is their home. This is a good time for them to learn to share and bring pleasure to others.

If there are some children in your group who do not have parents with them, the cell group should ask someone to be an adopted aunt or uncle to them. This means they will have a special role in helping the children fit into the group. The aunt or uncle would need to meet the natural parents of the children to start to build friendship and to seek their cooperation. Try to be especially sensitive to these children. Because they come from a home which has different values, they may make unintentional mistakes. They will also bring their own special blessing.

Lord,
We have willingly offered our home for You to use. It is precious to us as a family, but we want You to be able to use it. Help us to make it easy for other families to come into our home and feel comfortable. Help us to be warm and welcoming just as you were welcomed into the home in Bethany. Use our home as a place where your church gathers in our area and let us find joy in sharing it.

Amen

A Note to the Children's Coordinator

What kind of job is this?
Will I get help when I need it?
Who do I report to?

Dear Children's Coordinator:

Welcome to the job. You're probably feeling nervous already about the task you've taken on. Let me reassure you at once. You are not the one solely responsible for the children in the cell group. Their parents are there. Other members of the group are taking turns to lead the Kids' Slot. You should not be taking more turns than anyone else.

However, someone has to be the organizer for the team, and that's you. To sum it up briefly, you need to arrange the days on which the rostered members lead the Kids' Slot. If they have to be away unexpectedly they can swap with someone else. You may find that some group members are unwilling to do it alone but are willing to have a partner. You should aim at having at least 5–6 leaders so that no one has to do it more than once a month. Give everyone a written copy of the roster so they have plenty of advance notice.

Let people see this task as a commitment and promise to the Lord. If they think of it as just "babysitting" they will easily find excuses not to do it. Encourage them to **like** the children.

Why not import someone to look after the children? It's too easy to hand the children over to a "professional" and shrug off our own responsibility for them. The children need community – to be part of the cell group. Children know when someone is just "babysitting". If, however, there is a large number of toddlers in the group who require close attention, it would be possible to import some extra help.

Also consult with the Cell Group Leader about the weeks when the cell group doesn't meet. It's not fair for the children's leader to prepare something and find it's not needed.

Material for the Kids' Slot will be supplied to you by the Children's Ministry Leaders. You will get it well in advance so that you can make preparations early. Mostly, it will be picking up the theme of the worship and the teaching the children have had that Sunday. **It is not another teaching time for the children.** Rather, it is a time to talk about the issues that arise from the teaching, to work out some practical action, to make activity projects which support the theme and to revise the memory verse. It is supposed to be fun!

It's all right to include games, jigsaws, dressing up or any other things the children can enjoy together. There will also be time for the children to talk about some of the things that worry them. Children should learn to pray for one another and to help each other in times of need.

There should also be a time when the children plan an action for the next week. The action should arise out of the theme of the message. They may plan to speak to a child they do not know well. Or they may plan to do their chores without being asked. Or they may plan to visit an Old People's Home, or they may want to write to a friend or relative who is far away. The following week the next Leader should check to see whether they did it. This means that Leaders will need to write down the prayer needs and the planned action in a notebook which can be handed on to the next Leader.

Children should also learn to pray for friends and family who do not know Jesus. This constant reminder helps them to be aware of opportunities to include non-Christians in cell group activities.

It would be wonderful to have a time when the children pray for other people in the world – missionaries, distressed people, people who do not know Jesus. It would be good to have a scrapbook where you can keep maps and pictures. Children can be great prayer warriors.

One of the best things to do is to prepare something which they can use in the worship time with the adults. There may be others in the community that they can bless too. Encourage them to think of others.

Ask some of the older children to help plan ideas. They will come up with some neat suggestions and they would really work at something they've thought of themselves.

The weekly report is a bit of a chore and people hate handing in forms, but it is really important in Intergenerational Cell Groups. Without the weekly report forms, it would be easy for the Children's Ministry Leaders to lose touch with the children. The Children's Ministry would like to know who attends the Intergenerational Cell Groups, what is happening in their spiritual lives, what needs are surfacing and how the material is being used. Otherwise they could be working in a vacuum and have no idea of what is going on. Keeping good records is part of ministry. Good shepherds know their sheep.

You would be wise to meet with all your helpers occasionally. This will give you a chance to find out how they're doing and to prepare them for the next batch of material. Probably you will find that they have ways of helping each other. Use their skills and resources. Also you need to pray together.

Even though you are not the one solely responsible for the children there may be times when you would like to talk to someone. You can always call on a Children's Leader or IGC Facilitator to help you sort out a problem. You're not on your own. We find that problems are solved more quickly through prayer than anything else.

Do you want to pray now about this new responsibility?

> *Lord,*
> *I'm not sure what I've got myself into. I feel afraid that because I'm the leader of the team, I might be expected to do everything. Help me to trust the other people in the cell group and to share the difficulties with them. Help me not to do it alone and be too proud to ask for help. Thank you for calling me to this task.*
> *Amen*

Checklist for the Children's Coordinators

❏ Meet with the people on your roster to encourage them and to check that they know what to do. Some of them may want to sit in on a Kids' Slot before they try to lead it themselves.

❏ Check with the Cell Group Leader about which days there will need to be a Kids' Slot before making up your roster. Remind the helpers each week that it is their turn.

❏ Talk to Children's Ministry about collecting weekly material and handing in reports.

❏ Get a notebook to record prayer needs and also the actions the children plan to do during the week.

❏ Have a small activity for the children in case the cell group runs overtime – maybe a pack of cards or a puzzle. You might even keep a little thing to amuse a young child in case a mother gets frantic.

$\mathscr{A}$ Note to Children's Helpers

How should I prepare myself for the Kids' Slot?
What do I do when I get there?
How do I use the material I've been given?
How do I relate to the children?
How do I end the Kids' Slot?

Dear Children's Helpers:

So you've been brave enough to volunteer and you may still be wishing you hadn't. Ignore that feeling! That's the Devil trying to rob you of one of the great experiences of your life. It's understandable that you should be nervous about a new service to the Lord. But you don't need to be afraid.

"Where do I start?"

Children are not monsters! At least not unless we let them become one. They are people trying hard to be accepted and loved, trying to do the right thing and not to appear foolish, looking for friendship and approval – in fact, deep down they are a lot like you and me. The only difference is that they tend to show their feelings more.

When it is your turn to be on the Kids' Slot, **start praying for the children during the preceding week.** It's good if you know their names from the beginning. You need to know their names to establish good control. They don't respond to "Hey, You!"

Find out from the previous week's helper how things went. Were there things that needed follow-up? The previous leader should have written these things in **a notebook**; it will help you.

Was some activity left unfinished? Was some child sharing a need that should be remembered? Was there a question to be answered? Was there a behavior problem? If there were, you might want some help from your Coordinator or from the Children's Ministry.

Do not try to lead the Kids' Slot in your own strength. The children can tell when you are faking it. Your sense of inadequacy may be your best ally, as you rely on the Holy Spirit to give you wisdom and courage beyond your own.

Try to arrive at the home early so you can take a look at the area where the children will be. If there is anything you need, let your host know early. If there are things which are likely to distract the children, you can cover them with a sheet.

As soon as the children arrive at the Kids' Slot, have them sit in a circle on the floor. This is the easiest formation for control. If you allow them to sit on chairs or anywhere else, you cannot look them in the eye and you lose contact with them. Encourage the older ones to sit near the younger ones so they can help each other.

Enlist the support of any older children by giving them definite things to do. You may even phone them during the week so that they can be prepared. For instance, you might ask them to prepare some things for prayer or perhaps they could present the memory verse. Sometimes, children will prepare for a skit or role play. Younger children can distribute any required materials, like paper and pens or scissors.

Work your way through the material you have been given, but be flexible. If some things are not suitable for the children in your group, leave them out. You can substitute other ideas so long as you do things the children can get involved in.

Do not spend the whole session talking to the children and not letting them talk. They get very bored. If you find something in the material which doesn't work, note it in your report. Encourage them to make things or plan ideas to bless the adults. If you have finished the materials given, you can play any game, or just talk. It all builds relationships.

Let the children talk and make sure that you listen with your heart. Often a child will mention an important problem or question quite casually as though it didn't matter. They are too shy to say that it is important until they see how you react. They want to leave themselves space to withdraw if you react badly. Sometimes a child will be hurting badly underneath but they cover it with loud behavior and talk. The Holy Spirit will give you the discernment to know when to invite the child to talk further about a need. If you cannot meet their need yourself, talk later with the parents or the Cell Group Leader.

Let the children feel free to use spiritual gifts if they wish during the prayer time. However, do not let any children feel inferior because they do not exercise spiritual gifts. Explain that these gifts are open to anyone but that the Holy Spirit does not give every gift to everyone at the same time. If children wish to ask God for a spiritual gift you should talk to their parents and the Cell Group Leader.

Sometimes a child will choose to be uncooperative. There may be reasons for that. Perhaps they were in trouble before they left home and there is a bit of leftover rebellion in their hearts. Or they may feel neglected by the group, so they try to gain attention. If the children like and respect you, it is often enough simply to look them in the eye and ask them to cooperate.

We often find it helpful to pray aloud for a persistently troublesome child, or to pray for the group, asking a special blessing on the trouble makers. Scolding children or punishing them seldom works for long. Confrontation makes the session seem a burden to the children. If they love you, they will want to do what you say. If they do not, you should work at getting to know them. You could do something special to show that you appreciate them.

Time to Say "Goodbye"

Often in an Intergenerational Cell, it is hard to guess when it will end. You may be in the midst of a major project when the parents want to claim their children. Or you may be holding on to the children for an extra half hour while the parents continue talking. Everyone needs to understand this.

1. **When the children leave the adult group**, note the time and tell the adults when you plan to return – usually about 40–60 minutes later. The Cell Group Leader should note that and try to be ready for the children to return.

2. **When that time has come, send a child** to ask the Leader if it is all right for the children to return to the group. If not, you will need an extra activity to keep the children for a few minutes more.

3. **When they return to the adults, they should tell** the adults what they have been doing. One or two children can report on the Kids' Slot and show anything they have made. The adults should also report anything interesting to the children. If there is food the children should be encouraged to help serve the adults. They should not push in first.

Remember, your basic goal is to help the children practice and experience a full Christian life.

Encourage them in prayer.
Encourage them in the life of the Spirit.
Encourage them in reaching out to their friends.

Weekly Duties

1. Trust in God's power, not your own. Pray for the children.

2. Check whether there is anything you need to follow up from the previous week. Use your notebook.

3. Ask the children to help you.

4. Know the material and choose what you use.

5. Listen with your heart to discern the children's underlying needs.

6. Allow the children to exercise the spiritual gifts that the Holy Spirit has given them. Do not let the others feel inferior.

7. Deal with troublesome children with spiritual insight. Help them to obey you because they love you.

8. Plan the ending. You could hold hands and say a prayer of blessing.

9. Help them to make surprises to bless the adults.

10. Let them see the reality of your own faith and life.

Lord,
I believe you are asking me to lead these children this week. Help me to feel calm and relaxed and to enjoy them. There is nothing that You and I cannot handle together.

Amen

A NOTE TO THE FAMILY REPORTER

How do I find out about Family Events?
How much of the meeting should it take up?
Should I do anything extra
beyond the meeting?

Dear Family Reporter:

Congratulations! I think you have chosen the nicest job of all. It's such fun thinking up nice surprises for people. I know that both the children and the adults will look forward to your time in the cell group.

"Hold the tissue box! He's going to blow out the candles."

I guess you've already worked out how to remember people's birthdays. However, plenty of other good things happen in families. You can talk to the parents about what's happening to the children and the children may tell you about what's happening to the parents. New homes, new jobs, new schools, new babies, new grandparents, passing exams – they all need to be celebrated.

One of the best things to celebrate in a cell group is when one of the members gets baptized. It would be great if the children could be there to witness it. Maybe they could make a special card or a special gift to celebrate the occasion.

Of course, **you'll need to be sensitive** too. Sad things happen to people in life and they need to be able to grieve among their Christian friends. Even children have cause for grief – losing a friend or a pet, changing schools, failing in a test, having a grandparent die. You may be able to think of ways to show the love of the cell group to the child or the adult. It doesn't always have to be in the group. A phone call or a visit would be great.

There may be times when there's **a dull patch** and nothing seems to be happening. Or maybe there's some people in the group who always seem to be missed out. If that is so you could plan a special surprise recognition for something they're not expecting. That gives them a special sense of being loved.

Be creative in the things you do. Don't always just bring a card or a cake, though that can be nice. Keep in mind the person or the people you are planning the occasion for, and you can come up with something that suits their interests or personality, e.g., if a family is moving away from the city, give them a small album with photos of their own locality, or a notebook with a verse, or a thought from every cell group member, or the words of a favorite song written out nicely.

If you like making surprises for people, you're going to enjoy this task and the children will love you. When there are times of pain and disappointment for either the children or the adults, there is all the more need for a loving reassurance from the members of the cell group.

Louise had failed her college entry exam. No one expected it. No one knew what had gone wrong. Louise knew that on that day, her mind went blank and she couldn't think of what to write down. The doctor said it was stress.

Louise felt like a failure, but when she went to cell group there was a present for her – a book filled with messages from the members telling her how much she was appreciated. There was even a message from her teacher and her parents saying that they believed in her. Louise determined to try again.

Rejoice with those who rejoice and weep with those who weep!

$\mathscr{A}$ NOTE TO PARENTS

Will my child be a nuisance to the others?
What if my child misbehaves in the cell group?
Suppose I don't agree with other parents about discipline?
My child may reveal to the group things about our family.
What if my child doesn't want to go?

Dear Parents:

Perhaps you still have mixed feelings about Intergenerational Cell Groups. Inevitably, parents tend to think of the worst that could happen. That goes with the job.

Many parents are much more aware of their children's misdeeds than other people are. A child may be a little restless or wander around the group and the mother is constantly on the jump, trying to restrain him/her. The others can be more disturbed by the mother than by the child! If a child makes a mistake and accidentally breaks something, the father goes home angrily vowing never to take the child there again. He feels ashamed and embarrassed.

Many parents feel that their children are impossibly restless and cannot sit still. They feel upset because the child will not sit still and listen. Sitting still and listening is one of the hardest things we can ask children to do. They are filled with energy, so they will always tend to move and fidget.

However, in an Intergenerational Cell Group, we should not be asking children to sit still all the time. They can be active during the icebreaker and during the worship. They can dance and play instruments, hold up the song sheets, clap, raise their hands and do actions. When the group is praying, they should be praying too, laying hands on people, holding hands with a partner and sharing their needs. The children will certainly be active during the Kids' Slot and when they report to the cell group again, they will have something to show or talk about.

If the children are bored and restless in an Intergenerational Cell Group, it is because they are not being involved. We are boring them by ignoring them.

Most people understand that children are not perfect and will not always feel like cooperating. Adults have the same problem sometimes. When an adult feels like that, he does not need to be scolded, but to be encouraged and appreciated. The cell group should show love and acceptance to the children too. Too much scolding only makes the child feel unwanted and unloved in the group.

Some parents over-react because of their own feelings rather than because of the feelings of the group. This is because we are so anxious to give a good impression to other people that we often pretend that we do not have problems. Our children are supposed to reflect credit on their parents, not reveal problems.

Other parents tend not to notice what their children are doing. Once they enter the house, they forget about their children. Some even believe that their children should not be restrained in any way and they can be very defensive if their children are criticized. Which category do you belong?

Mark on this line where you fall on the area of discipline.

No discipline   *Heavy discipline*

←————————————————————————————→

1   2   3   4   5   6   7   8   9   10

The Bible is clear about how parents should behave towards their children. They should expect and receive obedience. When children obey their parents they are obeying God. On the other hand, parents should not exasperate their children or drive them into anger (Ephesians 6:1–4). There's to be a balance. Some parents are like see-saws, always falling in one direction or another.

Now suppose there are three families in the cell group and they are at different points in the discipline scale. How is that going to work?

When you realize the problem, you need to talk about it. The Cell Group Leader would be a good negotiator. Parents can be very sensitive about their children's upbringing because that represents all their values and their world view. But the cell group is the right place for talking about our life values. If you can talk in a non-threatening way about the things you expect from your children in the cell group, it should be possible to find an acceptable standard. It may even help some parents when they understand how other parents handle their children.

When both Mom and Dad are in the group, they should try to show unity in the way they handle the children. If the two parents come into conflict with each other, the children get confused and the other cell group members do not know whose signals to follow.

Parents should make sure their children understand that they are full members of the cell group. They should check that their children know about the House Rules. When the children go out to the Kids' Slot, they should let the children know that they should obey the leader.

Parents should not expect everything to go right all the time. Children are human, just like themselves. There will be times when children misbehave and they will be brought into line in the cell group. However, children should not be punished again when they go home. We do not want children to be afraid of coming to the cell group. Older children should not be blamed for the misbehavior of younger children. They do not have the authority to demand obedience. The best they can do is to report the bad behavior to their parents. They do not want to feel they are blamed for everything.

Ask for the Holy Spirit's guidance when you discuss the behavior of your children. It's an area which often grips our emotions. The Holy Spirit is the giver of peace and harmony, not heat and discord. He can help you be honest and loving at the same time.

What if the Children Don't Want to Come?

If you ask children whether they want to come to cell group, they will nearly always say "No". They think they are being asked to go to some boring adult meeting where they will be expected to sit still and be quiet all the time. We find that most children desire to come only after they have experienced what an Intergenerational Cell Group is like.

However, going to the cell group is not a thing which should be left to the children's choice. If the cell group is the church, then it is a family decision and the whole family goes. Parents do not give their children the option whether they should go to school, or whether they should brush their teeth. If you give your children the option whether they should go to church or to the cell group, you are silently telling them that God is not very important. If you do not insist on it, then worshiping God is an optional thing in life.

How Much Should You Share about Family Life?

Many parents would be surprised if they knew how much children tell their teachers about life in their family. Most teachers understand that this is privileged information and they are careful about what they hear.

In a cell group, it is quite possible that your child may reveal something you would prefer not to share with the group. Children say what they know and they don't think about privacy of information.

Some people are comfortable to be open about their home life. Others struggle with it. It's not fair to scold the child for telling the truth. If the whole cell group recognizes in advance that children can say embarrassing things, it will help everyone.

The Group Agreement requires both children and parents to ask permission before they tell personal family details. If a child does blurt out something you wish he hadn't, **don't panic.** Every family has problems and perhaps your openness will help some other family to share some of their problems too.

Don't muzzle your children so effectively that they are afraid to talk at all. Most family events can be shared with a cell group in a good spirit. People understand because they have problems too. In God's community, we can find release and support.

Children's secrets deserve the same respect. Parents can hurt their children by reporting things which the child thought were personal and private. Don't tell stories about your children just to win a laugh from the group. If the child is willing to share the incident, they will say so.

Karen had bought a cake for her mother's birthday using her own money. She planned to decorate it with strawberries and frosting and when she was finished she would sprinkle it with icing sugar. Unfortunately, she mistook the container and sprinkled the cake with baking soda. It tasted awful and she was so disappointed. Would you tell this story to the cell group?

Are the Children Too Busy?

Children today face great pressure of study and activities. We have a generation of "driven children" who are already showing signs of stress.

Cell group should not be an additional stress factor. It should be a place where a child can unload some worries and feel the love of God through the love of the cell group members. It comforts a child to know that adults are praying for him.

Besides, many children who honor God in their study patterns achieve better results than expected. God honors those who honor Him.

Telling the Children about IGCs

Merilyn took a deep breath and spoke to her son.

"Luke, did you know that our cell group is becoming intergenerational? That means that you and the other children will be coming too."

"You've got to be kidding! Who thought up that dumb idea? Honest, Mum, I don't want to go. They're your friends. I've got better things to do."

"Luke, you're not giving it a chance. This is something completely new. It's not just our old cell group doing its own thing. It's a new cell group with both children and adults as full members. We'll spend some of the time together and some of the time in our own groups. And it's not going to be like Sunday School either. It will be a real cell group and you'll be given a chance to help lead it. In fact, Keith our leader is hoping very much that you'll be on the leadership team for the Kids' Slot."

"Mum, I'm too busy. I've got so much study and tuition and then there is my athletics club. I don't want anything more."

Mum put her hand on Luke's shoulder. "I know, Luke, and I'm proud of you. But if you're too busy for God, you're too busy. Your father's busy too, but he still makes time for cell group. We've decided to do this as a family, and you're part of it. Come along to the meeting on Friday night and give it your best shot. This is really important to us."

Luke looked gloomy. "Who else is going to be there?" he asked.

"Well, Stephen will be there, and Lisa and their little brother. And of course you know Matthew, who works at the airline, and Sylvia's going to be the Children's Coordinator. You know Sylvia. She acted in that skit at the concert."

"Yeah, yeah", grunted Luke. "It might be all right. I guess I'll give it a try."

Lord,

You know that we are trying to be good parents and we know we often make mistakes. Help us to encourage our children more often than we scold them. Help us to learn from each other in the family, so that we do not pretend we know everything. When we discover we are wrong about something, give us the grace to say we are sorry, just as we teach our children to be sorry. Help us to respect our children and let them minister to us even as we care for them. We love our children and we want them to know through our lives that you love them too. Please help us, Lord.

Amen

The Role of the IGC (Intergenerational cell) Facilitator

*Who helps the cell groups make the transition to Intergenerational
Cell Groups?
How much outside help should the cell group receive?
Who supervises an Intergenerational Cell Group?
How do the Children's Coordinators receive support?*

When a church decides to transition into Intergenerational Cell Groups, many
people are confused about how to do it. The cell groups sometimes bring the
children in but do not know what to do with them. If the children are left to sit
still and watch, they rapidly become bored and they misbehave. Then the parents
keep their children away from the cell group. It's a vicious circle.

At the beginning of the process, the Children's Ministry Leaders should train
their existing leaders or other enthusiasts to become IGC Facilitators. These are
the people who will go into the cell groups in the first stages to lead the cell
group into the new format and to equip them to be able to handle it.

When a Cell Group Decides to be Intergenerational ...
The cell group invites an IGC Facilitator to visit their cell group to explain how
an IGC works and what they have to do. It seems ideal for the Facilitator to lead
the worship for that night and to run an icebreaker, just so that the parents can
see how the children respond. They will then give the little children an activity
while they talk with the parents. However, the older children often like to be
part of the discussion.

The Facilitator outlines for the cell group the program for the Intergenerational
Cell Group and the different roles which the people in the cell group have. They
also explain the Group Agreement and the House Rules. The adults in the cell
group will have a host of questions to ask and the Facilitator will need to be able
to help the parents understand the new paradigm in relation to their children.
This is often the hardest part of the process because so many parents have been
in the habit of passing their children over to someone else for teaching and nurture.

The Facilitator can encourage the cell group with stories of how the children have integrated into other cell groups and sometimes the Cell Leader will like to visit another group.

When the cell group decides to become an Intergenerational Cell Group, they will choose a Children's Coordinator and a Family Reporter and people will offer to be on the roster for leading the children. It is most important that the cell group does not leave it to one or two highly committed people. It is not fair for them to be cut off from the life of the cell group. Besides, the children need to get to know everyone in the cell group, if possible.

The First Stage of the Intergenerational Cell Group
The IGC Facilitator promises to stay with the cell group for at least four weeks.

Week 1
The Facilitator leads the cell group through the icebreaker, worship and the Kids' Slot.
The Children's Coordinator and one other person observe the Kids' Slot.

Week 2
The Cell Group Leader leads the worship and icebreaker.
The Children's Coordinator leads the Kids' Slot with another member observing.
The Facilitator also observes.

Week 3
The Cell Group Leader arranges the worship and icebreaker. The Facilitator may help with suggestions. Member A leads the Kids' Slot and Member B observes with the Facilitator.

Week 4
The Cell Group Leader arranges the worship and icebreaker. He may ask someone else to do them, if he wishes. Member B leads the Kids' Slot. Member C observes with the Facilitator.

The Facilitator will need to continue to feed ideas and materials to the Children's Helpers and worship leaders. This process will continue as the Children's Leaders service the group. Some Children's Coordinators are very good at coming up with their own ideas.

At the end of the four weeks the Facilitator will talk to the Children's Coordinator and the Cell Group Leader. If they feel confident, you could leave the IGC at this point and just keep in touch with the IGC's progress. If the leaders still feel insecure, you could stay with them for another two weeks. However, under no circumstances should the Facilitator stay with the group for longer than six weeks. If that happens, the adults in the cell group usually withdraw and become dependent on the Facilitator. The adults need to be encouraged into leadership as soon as possible. This is the only way they can feel the blessing of being with the children. The cell group can still phone the Facilitator and ask for help if a crisis arises.

When the Cell Group Is Fully Operational ...

If your cell group church has a network of Zone Supervisors and Zone Pastors, much of the reporting and accountability will still happen through the usual channels.

However, sometimes the Zone Pastors and Zone Supervisors feel inadequate to handle problems relating to the children. At this stage, they will like to have the help of the IGC Facilitators to give them advice and to help visit some cell groups.

The routine work of the IGC Facilitators will be to make sure that the cell groups are provided with weekly materials; to keep in touch with the Children's Coordinators; to encourage them; to draw them together from time to time to exchange skills and ideas with one another and to find the appropriate help if serious pastoral problems occur. They should also bring back to the Children's Leaders the good news of what is happening in the cell groups. Each Facilitator might have four or five Coordinators in their care.

When there are District events among the cell groups, the IGC Facilitators will help the leaders with ideas for involving the children. This would include prayer and praise nights, prayer walks, district camps, evangelistic events, community service, etc.

Children's Zone Pastor

Some Districts will be so large that they require a Children's Zone Pastor to lead the team of IGC Facilitators. They will encourage and supervise the Facilitators. Sometimes, they will provide training and extra resources for them. Sometimes, they will call them together to share experiences and to plan district events. The Children's Zone Pastor will also work alongside the other Zone Pastors in the district to help and advise them in all matters relating to the children. They should be fully part of the District reporting to the District Pastor.

Checklist for the Children's Facilitator/Pastor

Have I sensed God calling me into the work of being a Facilitator?

Have I studied the materials so that I understand the concept of the Intergenerational Cell Group?

Have I visited an Intergenerational Cell Group so that I have seen how it works?

Have I met with the Cell Leader and the potential Children's Coordinator to share the vision with them?

Have I prepared for the questions that the cell group is likely to ask?

Have I gathered some useful tools, such as percussion instruments, paper, colored pencils, games and the Kids' Slot materials?

Have I thought about how to lead worship with children so that I can model simple ways of involving the children?

Have I checked with the host so the Kids' Slot will have somewhere to meet?

Have I asked the Lord to go with me to help me talk with the cell group?

Part Three

THE PROCESS OF INTERGENERATIONAL
CELL GROUPS

*W*HAT HAPPENS IN THE KIDS' SLOT?

Is there a program and some materials?
How much preparation is involved?
How will I cope with mixed ages?
How do I keep control?
What am I trying to achieve?

Let's imagine that seven people offered to help lead the children for Kids' Slot. Two of them might prefer to work with a partner at first, which means that there would be a five-week roster.

At the beginning they would meet with a leader from the Children's Ministry to find out what happens in the Kids' Slot. This is a time to find out the details and ask any questions. They need to learn the regular structure before they start adding any other ideas. Kids' Slot is not intended to be rigid but if a person does not understand how the pattern works, they can try desperately to think of something new to do each week, and lose the basic concept of what a children's cell group is all about. Once the basic pattern is established, any number of ideas and variations are possible.

Some Things Happen with the Adults

A cell group program is sometimes summarized under four W's: Welcome, Worship, Word and Works. In an Intergenerational Cell Group, the first two W's usually take place while the children and the adults are together. This would include the icebreaker and the worship. There should also be some time when the children and adults share and pray together and when family events are recognized.

When the children arrive in the Kids' Slot, you can start with the first two W's if they haven't been covered already with the adults. Or you can even have a second icebreaker if you want to build more relationships. For instance, you might want a game to help you learn the children's names.

The Regular Structure

The usual events which take place in the Kids' Slot are Edification (the Word) and Sharing the Vision (Works). However, these can be expressed in four separate actions (outlined below). They do not always have to be in the same order. Sometimes, you might omit one or more of the actions. It's all right to be flexible.

These actions are at the heart of cell group life. Without this emphasis the cell group will drift back into being a class. The actions outlined here assume that the Bible teaching has been done elsewhere, probably in the Sunday celebration. If the teaching must be done in the cell group, it should be done in a relational and interactive way. It must be locked into the child's experience.

You could do it like this. Start talking with the children about life situation topics which lead into the biblical material. These topics are like a door into the story. You might talk about how it feels when no one likes you or wants to play with you. This could lead into the story of Zacchaeus. As you tell the story encourage the children to participate by asking them questions and engaging them in a conversation. Then you move into the four actions:

The Four Actions

Review (Word)

Review the theme which was taught on Sunday. If they found it boring, find out why. Let them explore the issues of the main theme. Let them ask questions which were not resolved. If there was a memory verse, the group could review it and perhaps do a role-play of a life situation when the verse would prove useful. Because the group has mixed ages, it means all the children should be following the same theme.

Report (Works)

Ask how the children succeeded in the action they planned last week, e.g., did they manage to avoid fighting with their brother or sister? Did they talk to a new friend they never knew? Were they able to read the Bible at least four times? Give thanks for their success and encourage those who found it hard.

Relaxation (Word)

Make or perform something which supports the teaching they received. This could be in the form of craft work, art, drama, music, dance, science, or anything else that occurs to you. Sometimes you can prepare a worship idea for the adults, or an act of service to someone who is in need, e.g., making scrapbooks for children in the hospital or for missionary children. Or they could write letters to lonely people.

Responsibility (Works)

The children can talk about friends or family members who do not know about Jesus. The children should pray regularly for these people and plan for ways to get to know them. Maybe the parents could help. If a new family joins the cell group, the children should learn how to welcome them and make them feel at home.

The children can pray systematically for their community and their leaders. They could plan some caring action to help other people in their world. They could also pray for missionaries and children in other parts of the world.

Be Doers, Not Hearers Only

We call these parts of the program, 'Action'. The emphasis in the Kids' Slot is on lifestyle rather than knowledge. Knowledge does not change their lives and attitudes. Children are 'doers' by nature. They learn best what they are able to put into practice.

The children will be helped in their actions by witnessing the actions of the adults. If they see adults reaching out to their friends, they will want to try it too. In fact, often children and adults can be effective when they work together.

If the children see adults striving to grow in their likeness to Jesus, the children will also follow their example. On the other hand, the adults can also be encouraged by seeing the enthusiasm of the children.

"Let me show you how to do it."

How to Lead the Four Actions

Review

You will be given an outline of the Sunday teaching and some questions to encourage the children to think through what the main issues were. You may even ask the children to tell the story to you and to any children who were not present on Sunday. You will also receive a copy of the memory verse to review. Some of the older children could do that. Try to get them to plan the action they would like to take as a result of the teaching e.g., "This week I will spend one hour playing with my baby sister."

Report

Help the children to report what has happened during the week. You may need to prompt them. "What happened at home? What happened at school? Did anything special happen? Was there something you were sad about?"

Ask the children to recall the actions they planned the previous week. Last week's Leader should have given you a notebook of the application shared by the children. Ask if the children have carried out what they had planned. Write down the action they planned for this week. Lead the children in praying for, and ministering to, one another.

Relaxation

Each week there will be suggested activities and resources. There is also a list in this book (See page 132). Help the children to prepare for coming events, e.g., the District Prayer and Praise Night, or the Easter Celebration. They can make displays or banners or pompoms or praise transparencies.

Responsibility

Encourage the children to show concern for others. Every child knows someone who does not know Jesus. They should be thinking of ways to bring that child a little closer to Him. We would like the children to be able to share John 3:16 with their friends and family. They may be able to invite their friends to some special event. Of course, this means that the children's lives will need to be consistent before their friends.

Children can be active prayer warriors. Teach them how to be alert to what Satan is doing in the world and how to pray against it. Children can learn to pray strategically, using a book called, *"You Can Change the World Through Prayer"* by Jill Johnstone. Also, there are good prayer tools available through the Esther Prayer Network in Florida (854 Conniston Road, West Palm Beach, FL33405, USA).

They should also be aware of the need in their own country and should pray for issues which concern them. They could even express their concern through writing to people who can do something about it. Make sure they know when God has won a victory. A prayer diary is a great help.

Other Activities You Can Use

1. Storytelling

Your cell group may be lucky enough to have some good storytellers. Children love to hear stories, not just Bible stories, but stories from life or from other books. You can encourage the children to talk about the story and to work out what it means. Don't tell them the meaning. They like to discover it for themselves. You can help them with clues, however.

2. Visitors

Children love to meet a new person who will talk to them about interesting things. The most ordinary person in a cell group or district will know of things that would interest children. An airline pilot could talk about his timetable and the places he flies to. What does he do all the time in the cockpit? How does he find his way about? A restaurant owner can talk about how he prepares the food and how he assesses the amount of ingredients he would need. Maybe he can talk about some of the funny things people ask for.

Most people have something in their lives which children would enjoy hearing – a hobby, a sport, something that happened when they were young. Children also like to meet people from another country.

3. Outings

The Kids' Slot does not always have to stay in the same place. The group could go for a walk or visit a nearby park. It is good to have a ratio of one leader to every 5–6 children. Older children are helpful in escorting the little ones. Make the walk more meaningful by looking for special things – colored leaves or odd-shaped stones.

A walk is not just for amusement. The children learn how to help and protect each other. There are strict rules about behavior. If you go to a park, you could have food, or act out a Bible story.

Learning doesn't have to come out of a book with everyone sitting down concentrating. Some of the best learning takes place when we are having fun together and when we are willing to hear what people are saying. For older children, learning to act responsibly towards the younger ones is a motivation towards spiritual growth.

4. Games

Playing games, whether indoors or outside is a good activity for the Kids' Slot. Games allow good interaction and the children have to relate to each other as they play together. They will need to make allowances for younger children and learn how to play fair, yet with mercy.

5. Food

Your Intergenerational Cell Group may be in the habit of eating together before they leave. If so, the children should join in. Sometimes children can enjoy eating while you are talking together. Keep it simple. Cut up an apple or an orange or share out some raisins. Popcorn is popular or cookies or potato chips but don't make it a party.

6. Cooking

Children love to do simple cooking. Sometimes you could bring a frying pan. Some cakes and sweets do not require cooking. The children love making these. And eating them!

Keep a Notebook!

Every leader should note down each week what happened in the Kids' Slot. There should be the planned action for the week. Prayer requests should be noted. Record the activity. It's easy to overlook things between two meetings, and this can be a disappointment to children.

Pastoral Problems

Sometimes in the Kids' Slot, children will tell you about what is distressing them. It can be anything from child abuse to bullying at school. Most people feel very inadequate to help the child.

1. Listen carefully to make sure you understand the problem. Do not force them to talk about it to the other children if they are not willing to do so.
2. Pray hard. If the child trusts you enough to tell you a problem, you need God's help to find an answer.
3. You could talk to the parents, or the Cell Group Leader. Ask the child's permission first, however. You can get help from the Children's Ministry staff. Or the child may just need someone to listen to him.

$\mathscr{B}$ABIES AND TODDLERS

What do we do with babies and toddlers?
How do we cope with feeding and sleeping schedules?
Will the toddlers be a distraction to the group?
Do these little children really benefit by being there?

Sandra phoned Sylvia during the week before the first IGC meeting:

"Sylvia, I'm really concerned about my two little ones in the cell group. I know the parents are supposed to keep them in the group, but I'm afraid it's just going to spoil the group for me. Don't you think we could send them out with the other children?"

"Well, we do have a problem there, Sandra," replied Sylvia. "During the Kids' Slot we are trying to run a genuine children's cell group and it's very hard for little children to be able to join in. They have such a short attention span. However, I don't really think that it will disturb the people if your little ones play quietly or wander about. Maybe we should try it out. Have you talked to Keith about this?"

"Yes, I have," answered Sandra. "He feels sure the group can cope with them but I don't know. I can't cope with them myself at home sometimes."

About a week later Sandra called Sylvia again:

"I'm just so excited about what happened at the IGC," she bubbled over the phone.

"I would never have believed it. I mean I just fed the baby and she settled down to sleep in her crib and as for Samuel, he was as good as gold. He just loved that tambourine that Keith gave him to play with."

"I know," laughed Sylvia. "He looked so cute sitting there solemnly banging his tambourine while we sang. He really seemed to get into the spirit of the thing. Even when we were sharing and praying, he just wandered around the group quietly and finally ended up on his Daddy's knees.

"I was really surprised by the new lady, Rose. She had that little cardboard puzzle in her bag and she kept him occupied for ages with it. She even seemed to keep track of the conversation at the same time."

"I think she was a schoolteacher once," suggested Sylvia, "and I know she has two grandchildren of her own."

"Well, she was a real blessing to me," said Sandra.

A few weeks later, Samuel started going to the Kids' Slot with the other children. One of the older children adopted him.

Do you have any older people in the group who have some experience with children? Spiritual grandparents have a special ministry with the children.

Toddlers Wear Their Mothers Out

Living with an active toddler all day is very tiring. Even coming home from work and dealing with a small child can sap all your energy. That's why many mothers would rather cope at home rather than make the effort to take their toddler out to cell group. Fathers often arrive home so late that they can't help much. Does it really matter if the little ones are not there? Don't the mothers need a rest?

God Enjoys the Praises of the Children and Their Parents

Of course little children can praise God anywhere, but I believe God enjoys the praises of little children in a cell group. We are the ones who have the problems. If all the toddlers are left at home they do not get to know their spiritual family.

"At that time Jesus, full of joy through the Holy Spirit, said, 'I praise you, Father, Lord of heaven and earth, because you have hidden these things from the wise and learned, and revealed them to little children. Yes, Father, for this was your good pleasure.' " Luke 10:21

Sadly in some homes the children do not learn to praise at all. God planned for babies and infants to praise Him (Psalms 8:2). The cell group is a good place for them to learn how to worship. Parents see how other parents teach their children to praise and worship. They may even learn to help their children to praise and pray at home.

However, mothers need to be able to praise and worship too. Sometimes, they will stay home with their babies, feeling tired and depressed, when they really need the encouragement of the cell group supporting them in their important task. This is especially true of single parents. If two-parent families refuse to bring their young children to the cell group, single parents feel their young children are not welcome in the group either. Two parents may take turns to baby-sit their children but a single parent would be excluded from the group altogether.

Every parent is a novice in bringing up children. Even the third or fourth child is always different. When parents do not understand their children's behavior they begin to wonder if they are normal. In the cell group they are reassured as they see other families cope with their children. They can also tap into fresh resources from God.

The Fast-Moving Agenda of Toddlers

Toddlers in a cell group are able to participate at their level. There is usually something they can do which is part of the action. The real difficulty is that their agenda is more fast-moving than ours. Because their attention span is so short, they get bored with what the grown-ups are doing. They look for fresh fields to conquer.

Adults find this annoying and the toddlers are blissfully unaware of the problem they are causing. The chief characteristic of this age-group is self-focus. They are not aware of other people's feelings or needs. They carry on doing what they are doing and they are amazed when anybody objects. They cannot understand why they are being checked.

Young children also have a fairly orderly routine. When feeding time comes, they are hungry and they are not inclined to wait. When they are sleepy, they will sleep – anywhere!

This means that the cell-group needs to be fairly accommodating. The little babies may need to be fed during the group meeting. A child may fall asleep. Another child may wander about, joining the action for some time and then following his own concerns.

It is not essential for children to sit still throughout the cell group meeting. They may wander from person to person and visit with a new friend for a few minutes, but they usually go back to the parents soon. The cell group should have some toys or objects available for the children to play with. Children are often more interested in safe ordinary objects than they are in toys. Empty grocery packets can be re-sealed. Colored plastic bottles can be cleaned and closed. Children can be delighted with large buttons or a mirror or a comb. If you cut up plastic drinking straws, little children can thread them on a string.

The best toys include things like a kaleidoscope, simple drawing toys, simple jigsaws and blocks. Avoid toys which require great movement – such as dump trucks and balloons. Some adults always try to keep some objects that amuse a toddler in their bag. It is good for a child to learn the discipline of playing quietly in a group.

On the other hand, children will often continue to play for a long time if they are given occasional encouragement. Recently I had some children draw a picture of the people in the cell group. This included two-year-olds. They were occupied for an hour-and-a-half, with only occasional interruptions to show off their work.

Other People Care
It's amazing how much the others are blessed by your children. People who have no other contact with children often like to see the younger ones and they can be very tolerant. It does not bother them to have young children moving about quietly even when the discussion is going on. I love to see little children making friends with adults in the group.

Of course if children are distressed, one parent probably needs to settle them down in another room, but ordinary baby noises and gurgles are not disturbances. I believe God even enjoys them!

Pre-Cell Groups
In another cell group there might be seven children under the age of three and no older ones. It would seem almost impossible to run the Kids' Slot time if all the children are too young.

These children form a special group because of their age, but that doesn't mean that they should be left out. They can still worship very well. Because they cannot yet read, we can make up scrapbooks which illustrate the words of the songs, or cards which they can hold up as the appropriate words are being sung. They can wave cheer pompoms or flags. They love percussion instruments. You can pray for them and get them praying in various ways. They can sing prayers, recite prayers, or place their hands on others to pray.

Some groups may like to bring in someone to look after these children during the cell group. If you do that the children do not get a chance to know the cell group members and they wouldn't feel like part of the family. These children grow very quickly and soon they will be old enough to be part of the cell group. It is much harder to bring them in when the parents have become accustomed to having a babysitter.

However, if there are so many toddlers that it is difficult for one person to manage, it would be possible to bring in one helper from outside the group. It could even be a teenager.

If most of the children in the cell group are toddlers, your Kids' Slot may take the form of a Pre-Cell Group. This is not a full cell group since it omits the dimensions of accountability and evangelism. The children will not be able to discuss questions logically. However, they love to play "Let's Pretend" games and their learning and discussion arises out of their play.

These children can respond to stories and music, creative play, movement and games. Often children will tell a soft toy how they are feeling or they will show love to the toy. They can learn how to do things together, how to share, how to care about others and how to take turns. It will prepare them for future cell group life.

Don't overlook the men in planning the leaders for this group. Many men love to get to know little children in a safe context. They can work with a partner to get to know and experience small children. For many small children, it is often a great joy for them to have a man as a friend. Their Daddies are absent so often that they love to play with someone strong. Make sure you protect the children and the men by having more than one leader.

Portrait of a Pre-Cell Group

Helen looked around the room at seven toddlers and wondered why she'd offered to look after them. She was 19 and a trainee teacher so the cell group thought she needed the experience. She felt very inadequate. "Lord," she prayed under her breath, "it's just You and me this time, and You need to come through for me."

Actually she did have another helper. Philippa, aged 14, had offered to help and that was good because right now little Michael was bawling vigorously. The others were just letting off steam after being with the adults for 40 minutes.

Helen sat on the mat and picked up her guitar. She began to strum some chords and she started singing, "This is the day that the Lord has made." The children came over to see what was going on. As they arrived, she gave each child a shaker or a bell so they could make music. Even Michael stopped crying when he saw what was happening.

"Start clapping," called Helen to Philippa. "Give it a strong beat." The children soon picked up the beat and then Helen moved to a new song.

"Let's do actions," she said. "Stand up everyone." The whole group began bending and stretching and raising their arms, following Helen's movements; all, except Michael who was still sobbing occasionally and Amy, who stood watching with her thumb in her mouth.

With Philippa's help Helen organized the children into a line and started walking round the room as they sang. She began to think of different things they could do.

"I'm going to zoom, zoom, zoom around the room, room, room. I'm going to zoom around the room and praise the Lord."

Suddenly she wondered if the noise was disturbing the adults. Just as well, the children had removed their shoes.

Before long Helen sat them down on the mat. It was time to play "Families".

"Let's play mothers and fathers", she suggested. "Father has to go off to work. Anthony, would you like to be father going to work? Here's your bag to put your lunch in.

"Mommy isn't going to work today. She's going to do the washing. What a lot of washing Mommy has to do. How big is the pile? Wow! So big! All right, Colette. You pretend to be Mommy doing the washing.

"Who can be the baby? Michael? I don't think he feels like it yet. Let's try Simon. What should the baby do? Oh, the baby has just fallen over and hurt his knee! Poor Simon is crying. What should Mommy do? What would your Mommy do, Colette?

"Find a plaster and put it on? Well, that's a good idea. What else could we do? Anthony you're supposed to be at work. All right Anthony, what would your Mommy do? She'd pray? What a good idea. Let's pray for Simon's poor leg. Lord Jesus, we know that you love us. Please help Simon's leg get better."

"Look! It's better," shouted Simon.

"That was just pretend," said Lorin. "It didn't really hurt."

"But Jesus can make my knee better when I really hurt it," declared Anthony.

"I had a cold and Jesus made it better," added Colette.

"And I... I... " Amy was trying to say something but she gave up.

"She wants to say that she had a cold too," said Colette, her sister.

"Does Jesus really make people better?" asked Helen.

All except Lorin nodded firmly. "Not right at that moment," added Anthony. "Sometimes you have to wait."

"I know a story about a man in the Bible who was very sick and Jesus made him better," said Helen. At this moment Michael decided to go wandering down the stairs, but Philippa followed behind him and brought him back. She picked up a mirror from the play-box and began playing with him.

"This man was sick all over," continued Helen, "especially his arms and legs. He had big white spots on his skin. Let's rub our arms and our legs where the spots are." All the children copied Helen vigorously rubbing their arms and legs.

"I've had measles and my spots were itchy too," said Simon.

"I'm sure you weren't allowed to play with your friends either, Simon," said Helen. "This poor man couldn't go near anyone because they might get sick too. It's horrid being sick all on your own. One day someone told him, 'Jesus can make you better if you go to see Him.' Who would like to say that? Lorin?"

"Jesus can make you better if you go to see Him," said Lorin.

"All right," said Helen. "Let's go to see Jesus. Everyone get up and walk in a circle round the room until we find Him. My, we've got a long way to go. Look there He is, over there. Philippa, you pretend to be Jesus. What should we say to Jesus now that we've come all this long way?"

"Jesus, please make me better?," suggested Anthony.

"Yes, that's good, Anthony. What this man actually said was, 'I know you can make me better if you want to.'"

"Did Jesus want to?" asked Lorin.

"Yes he did," answered Helen. "He reached out His hand and touched the man and said, 'Be well again,' and straightaway the spots disappeared.

"Philippa, you touch everyone one of us and say, 'Be well again.'"

"My Mommy had a bad headache before she came tonight," said Lorin. "Could Jesus make her better again?"

"Yes he can," said Colette. "'Cos my Mommy had a bad pain last week and I prayed for her and she got better."

Helen gathered the children in a circle and they held hands.

"Lord Jesus, we all want to pray for Lorin's Mommy and we ask that you will heal her bad headache."

"And my Grandma too," added Simon. "She's sick."

"And Simon's Grandma too," added Helen. "Please make her better soon."

"And my cat," cried Anthony. "She's going to have kittens soon."

"Lord Jesus, please let Anthony's cat have some beautiful kittens soon," said Helen obediently. "And let Anthony be able to enjoy them."

By the time they had finished praying, Helen reached for the face paint she had brought along to paint spots on the children's arms and legs. However, it was getting late. The adults were breaking up their group. She hurried to put a little paint on each child's face so they could show their parents. Suddenly Anthony said, "I was the father and I never came home from work!"

"You're right – you didn't! You'd better come home now. What do you say when you get home?"

"Hi, darling, I'm home!" said Anthony.

"That's great," said Helen. "You're a good kind of father."

As Helen tidied up she felt a sense of relief. She'd survived! She'd even quite enjoyed it. She felt she'd learned a lot about the children. She laughed when she remembered Anthony. Next time she'd use the face paint earlier and maybe involve Philippa a bit more. Also, she'd like someone else to play the guitar, or perhaps she could bring along a tape recorder.

When Lorin got home, she said, "Mom, we all prayed for you so now you're going to get better." And Mommy did.

Evaluation

Playing families (or any other life experience game) is a good way of modelling real life situations and talking about values. Often as the children play they will share with you things that worry or delight them. The play is not random. The Leader guides it in the desired direction and lets the children explore the ideas. The children are quick to follow their Leader and they love to act out adult behavior.

Often you can move from the play conversation into the Biblical material without a noticeable break. Children want to compare things that happen in the Bible with things that happen to them. Because little children are unashamedly self-focused, they always relate back to the things they know. This is a wonderful opportunity to apply Biblical truth to actual situations.

The pre-cell group emphasized the effectiveness of prayer. Some people are afraid that this will eventually lead to disillusionment when children's prayers do not get answered. This doesn't worry me. God is kind enough to answer the prayers of children many times and He loves their faith. When their prayer is not answered, that is a "teachable moment". The group can talk about it and work out why God didn't answer their prayer at that time. Children need to discover that God is a Father and not a magician. Sometimes He says, "No." We can help the child to meet with disappointments without losing faith.

It would be far worse for a child to grow up too afraid to ask God for anything. How sad that some people never even try God's power!

TRAINING PEOPLE FOR INTERGENERATIONAL CELL GROUPS

How much training do the helpers need?
What do the helpers need to know?
When and where should people be trained?

Most people who work in Intergenerational Cell Groups look for some form of training. This is natural and praiseworthy and the church should try to help them. There is one minor problem. Some of the blessing of the Intergenerational Cell comes from the fact that the people are not professional child-carers. They are ordinary people who love children but who make mistakes from time to time. Children trust people who love them for their own sake and not as a profession.

There is no guaranteed way of leading children. Each Leader develops a personal style and the children seem to enjoy the variety. God uses each Leader within the skills of their own personality. He *really* does take our weaknesses and use them beyond all that we could imagine.

The Basic Requirements

There are basic ideas which will make the task easier for everyone. The coordinators and helpers do not need a full course on teacher training. They need to know how to relate to children. They need to understand clearly what they are trying to do. They must be humble enough to learn from children. You can learn about children as you get to know them and talk with them. The basic ideas of child development can be learned in an afternoon. Watching how they work out may take a lifetime.

The content of the cell group is not nearly as important as the relationship. God uses relationships to produce radical change in the lives of the children. One of the most important things you need when working with children is the ability to relax with them. Children cannot trust people who are remote and formal. They need people who can laugh and play and tell stories and be open and forgiving. You do not lose control when you relax. Children learn to love you and therefore respect you. You do not win respect by demanding it. You have to earn it.

These are some of the basics to ensure effective leadership in an Intergenerational Cell Group:

1. The Difference Between a Cell Group and a Classroom

As long as the leaders model their leadership on a remembered Sunday School program they will never achieve a cell group. They need to think, work, speak and practice cell group until it is part of their being. The Leaders are members of the children's cell group, not outside of it. Both the children and the Leaders are members of the body of Christ. They can minister to one another.

School teachers often find it harder to create this atmosphere because they are accustomed to a classroom environment. Many good schoolteachers are happy to be able to relate to the children on a more human basis. Parents who have good relationships with their children will find it easy. People who try to impose rigid control on children will struggle with the concept. The children will adapt readily to a cell group pattern. They are very flexible. It is often the adults who find it difficult.

Many of the problems arise from the fear that the children will perceive the relaxed atmosphere as weakness. The cell group does not lack control, but it uses a different kind of control based on friendship and respect.

2. Techniques of Relating to Children

Many adults find it hard to start a friendship with a child. They have forgotten how a child thinks. They try to talk down to the child as if they were talking to a lesser being. Children can soon tell when an adult does not respect them.

Adults should relate to the children on the same basis as they relate to another adult. They should show respect for the children and listen to what they say. They should find something in a child's life which is of common interest so they have something to talk about together. They should listen to the child's 'story' and know a little of the child's life and background. They should be able to share their own background with the children and tell stories from their own life. The Leader should affirm the children and let them know that they are accepted in the group. Even if the children are uncooperative at times, the Leader will not help the children by rejecting them. Children will want to follow a Leader whom they love.

When children grow to like you, they will trust you with important secrets. These may not always seem important to you, but the child regards them seriously. Leaders should never betray the confidence of a child. They will never trust you again. If a secret is so serious that it must be shared with the child's parents or some other responsible person, Leaders must gain the child's permission before they speak. At the very least, they must explain to the child why they need to tell someone about it. Often, with the Leader's support, children can be encouraged to tell the secret themselves.

The more you talk with the children, the more they will grow to love you. It doesn't take hours. If a Leader can remember the children's names and greet them when he/she sees them outside the cell group, the children feel warm and loved. When a Leader remembers the children's birthdays or phones up when they are sick, he/she becomes a very special person in the child's life.

When you have a child as your friend, you are building a bridge across the generations. There is a special blessing in that.

3. A Brief Understanding of Child Development
This does not require a college degree! For cell groups the Leaders need to be reminded how much they have changed since they were children. Once you have entered a later stage of life, it is hard even to recall the way you used to think.

In summary, the stages can be described like this:

Babies and toddlers discover the world through touch and movement. That is how they explore life and find out facts.

From two to seven years, children are governed by their imaginations. They live in a world of endless mystery and possibilities. They believe what they are told without understanding it or questioning it. They have not yet learned to find reasons or causes. They are unimpressed by facts. They live in an imaginary world where anything can happen. Their attention span is very short.

From seven to 12 years, they move into a world of facts and developing reason. They often reject the imaginary. They only want to know things that are 'really true', that is, things that are tangible and visible. They are not yet able to cope with abstract thought. Their mental world is very literal, concrete and present. They cannot understand metaphors and symbols. They like to know about things that are happening in the world now. Last week is history.

Around the age of 13 years, children learn to understand abstract concepts and to deal with life issues. They realize there are deeper problems in the world than just superficial facts.

Children can reach God in any one of these stages. Relationship is a spiritual concern and even little children can relate to someone they love. Cell group helpers need to learn that little children learn through imagination. School-age children want plenty of facts and will ask many questions. Older children usually want to know the concepts behind the facts. All this is possible in an Intergenerational Cell Group. There is likely to be someone in the cell group who can answer the awkward questions. The older children can even help the younger children with their problems.

4. Group Management Skills

Group dynamics work the same way for children as they do for adults. One child will talk a lot to gain attention. Quiet children will not say anything until they feel it is safe. Children have a good sense of justice and they will want to stop one child from dominating the conversation, or from interrupting other people when they are speaking. One of the guidelines in the Group Agreement should be that people do not interrupt when another person is talking.

Leaders should make sure that every child has an opportunity to talk. Some children find it hard to break into a fast conversation, so the Leader should make space for them. People do not have to talk all the time. It is good sometimes to have a pause for reflection.

Leaders need to learn how to use their eyes. With our eyes we show concern, attention, warning, and even laughter. All our emotions show through our eyes and the children watch us to see how we are responding. Leaders who gaze over the children's heads, or plunge their eyes into a book, have little hope of controlling the group.

To encourage participation, look directly at the child you hope will answer the question you asked. If they do not respond you could say, "James, what do you think about that?" Then throw it open for other children to respond. Leaders are there to facilitate the conversation, not to dominate it.

Children like to know there is a basic structure to the group so they know what to expect. If they have a part in leading the group, they are much more willing to cooperate. Often the older children will help to control the younger ones. Even a small child likes to be given something to do. They may be put in charge of handing out the pencils, for example.

5. Learning to Handle the Group Structures

The Leaders should have the cell group agenda firmly fixed in their minds, not as a cage but as a guideline. One useful structure is the 4 W's: Welcome, Worship, Word and Works. All the basic activities come under one of these headings.

It is not a sin to leave out some activities on any particular night, if a problem arises. You can also include some other activities if you have a time gap. However, the basic ingredients create the character of the cell group. If you leave them out for too long you will change the nature of the cell group. It is good for helpers to watch other people doing the Kids' Slot so that they see how the parts fit together.

The lesson materials tend to influence the character of the group. As long as it is written in a leader's manual, most helpers will follow the lesson material even if it is not designed for cell groups. If you are not using cell group materials, the staff or supervisor should help the leaders adapt traditional lesson material.

Urge the leaders to leave their lesson materials at home, or keep them out of sight during the Kids' Slot. They can refer to it if they need to, but the children need to see that the message is coming from the leader's heart.

6. Intercession – Winning the Battle through Prayer

People often take prayer for granted – and then they don't do it! If a group is having problems, sustained prayer may be the answer. Satan loves to upset and distract the children. He can use any minor disturbance. This makes the leader feel useless so they want to give up and then Satan wins a victory. Signs of Satan's attacks are: grumbling, disorder, inattention, conflict, loneliness, aggression, selfishness, rejection and random noise. These problems can break down the trust of the group very rapidly. The children ride on the crest of the noise and the leader feels helpless.

This is the moment when the leader should take control through prayer, and banish Satan from their midst. They should encourage the children to recognize what is happening and to join hands in asking the Holy Spirit to bring peace and harmony.

No one in the team should see the Kids' Slot as babysitting. That is one of Satan's favorite lies. As long as the leaders think like that, they will be waiting for the time to be over. If they see the children as their friends, they will be trying to help them grow as the children of the Kingdom.

Times and Places for Training

The best kind of training happens on the job through observing other Leaders. Initially this may be difficult while everyone is learning but later every new helper should have the chance to watch someone else before they start leading themselves.

When the Intergenerational Cell Group is set up there should be some initial training to introduce the ideas. Various members of the cell group should study the notes addressed particularly to them and they should have the chance to respond. Perhaps a few weeks into the Intergenerational Cell Group and they should have the chance to report their blessings and problems.

The group should not try to solve every problem before it happens. Some people want to know answers to questions which may never arise. The best way of learning is by doing.

There is great value in having the children's helpers meet from time to time, especially when a new unit is being introduced. This helps them to share ideas and resources, to plan who should do what section, to spread the materials over the available weeks and to work out any group projects. Sometimes, there could be a fun session when everyone learns some new skills in drama, crafts or activities. It should also be a time for praise and intercession, as everyone gives the glory back to God.

*T*HE CELL GROUP WORSHIPS TOGETHER

Can children really worship the Lord, or do they just sing?
How can we involve the children in worship?
Will children be able to speak words from the Lord?

"*Yeh! Jesus!*"

Most people feel nervous when they introduce children into the worship. They are afraid the worship will be dominated by the children. No one in the cell group really wants to worship at 'kiddy' level, not even the children. They like fun songs at times, but they also like to sing praises to God with their whole hearts. On the whole, they prefer the songs the grown-ups sing, even if they don't always understand them. Have you noticed how even little children like to sing the 'pop' songs? Older children resent being asked to sing songs which belong in the nursery. You will be surprised to witness the sincerity with which the children approach God.

Helping Children to Worship

Children, especially boys, are often reluctant to sing loudly. They feel self-conscious. They like to know that everyone is joining in. We can help them by providing percussion instruments for them to play. If some children are learning music and have a portable instrument, like a flute or a violin or a recorder, they should be encouraged to bring it to the cell group.

Children enjoy praise songs but sometimes they misunderstand the language. During the interlude, it is helpful to explain what some of the songs mean. This can be helpful to many adults too.

Encourage the children to prepare some worship ideas for the cell group. They can teach a new song, or dance or draw a praise picture, or teach the adults some sign language. They can always use their memory verse to praise God.

Children Can Hear God's Voice

If your group spends some time listening to the Lord's voice and sharing it with the group, allow the children to do it too. They can speak words of blessing to the group but they need to know that they have permission. Be patient enough to let them explain what they mean.

One six-year-old boy wanted to tell the group about his word from the Lord. He stood up and rambled about monsters. People began to get restless. At last a leader took the boy aside and talked with him. In a few minutes they came back and she explained what he was trying to say.

"I saw a monster who was doing all the bad things in the world and I wanted to go out to fight that monster."

"Aren't you afraid to fight a monster like that?" asked the leader.

"I'm not afraid," he said. "I've got Jesus on my side."

Often children will share a word from the Scriptures and this will also bless the adults. It is often a good idea for the children to whisper their 'word' to a leader before they speak it to the whole cell group.

Worship Ideas

1. Tell a little background to the song.
   E.g., "Therefore the redeemed of the Lord shall return."
   The song tells of the promise to the exiles that they will return to Jerusalem and all their sadness over being captives will disappear. What might this song mean to us?

2. Use the prayer between songs to explain any symbols in the song.
   E.g., "For you are the great High Priest."
   The High Priest was the leader of Israel who entered into the Holy of Holies once a year to seek forgiveness for the people. Jesus is the great High Priest, who can bring us forgiveness every day.

3. Explain the difficult words.
   E.g., Jehovah Jireh means 'The Lord our Provider'. It comes from the time when Abraham was offering Isaac as a sacrifice to God but God provided a lamb to be the sacrifice instead.
   E.g., "Sacrifice of praise" means offering our songs to God because they will bring Him pleasure.
   E.g., "fruit of our lips" means the things we say and sing.

4. Ask people including the children to bring a song which is special to them. Let them explain why it is special.

5. Ask people to bring an object which reminds them of something they would like to offer to God in their lives.

6. Use a picture to reflect the mood or the language of the song. Let the group reflect on the picture before they sing.

7. Tell something about the circumstances in which the song was written. How did the writer feel? E.g., "It is well with my soul."

8. Ask the children and adults to close their eyes and imagine the picture which the song has just described. Let them offer words of thanks or praise.

9. Use sign language which is an expressive way of interpreting a worship song.

The chief priests and the teachers of the law became angry when they saw the wonderful things he was doing and the children shouting in the Temple, "Praise to David's Son." So they asked Jesus, "Do you hear what they are saying?"

"Indeed I do," answered Jesus. "Haven't you read this Scripture? 'You have trained children and babies to offer perfect praise.'"
Matthew 21:15–16

*S*haring and Praying with Children

Can children share their needs in front of adults?
How effective is the prayer life of a child?
Can children pray in the Spirit?
How can we help children to pray?

Encouraging Children to Share

Often children are too shy to share at their first meeting. They feel awed by the presence of the adults and they are not sure how the adults will respond. Most children prefer to talk about their problems among themselves but this way they do not get very good advice.

When children have the courage to share something from their lives, they need to be accepted, even if it is something quite trivial. They have taken a risk and that deserves praise. If they are ignored or made to appear foolish, they will not take the risk again.

Be patient with the children. When they see you sharing your news and praying for each other they will want to do it too. They learn from your willingness to talk about what happens in your lives. Sometimes they are reluctant to talk because children are supposed to be quiet when grown-ups are around. They cannot really trust you not to scold or criticize them.

Once you have established a pattern of sharing which includes the children, you may find some children go to the opposite extreme. They can be too keen to talk. Never allow a child to interrupt when someone else in the group is talking. If children demand too much attention after they have already had a turn, suggest quietly that other people need to have time to share too.

Sometimes parents will try to control their children's conversation in the cell group. This can be embarrassing if the group feels that the parents are trying to manipulate what the child wants to say. Parents may get a shock when a child reveals something they were not aware of, and they can try to argue with the child. It's usually better for the Cell Group Leader to guide the sharing. The children will respect the leader and they will usually cooperate.

The parents may want to talk further to the child when they get home but they should not punish a child for what they say in the cell group. Children should not be frightened into silence.

Children at Prayer

Write 'Yes' or 'No' after these statements.
1. Children will not pray in front of adults. _____
2. Children believe that their prayers will be answered. _____
3. Adults find it easier to pray than children do. _____
4. Children mostly ask God for things. _____
5. Children get bored if adults pray too long. _____

If you wrote 'Yes' for questions 2 and 5, you were right. Once children learn how to pray aloud, they have very few worries about praying in front of other people. They are far less inhibited than adults and they do not mind making a few mistakes.

Children do pray in faith. They believe in God's power to answer and they believe He will. Sometimes it is hard for them to understand why God does not answer every prayer. That's where they need the help of the adults in the cell group to explain why God cannot answer every prayer.

Adults generally find it harder to pray aloud than children do. They are more conscious of the other people and they worry that the others will think their prayer is not adequate. They feel shame if they make a mistake when talking to God.

Children can be trained to pray in every mode of prayer: adoration, confession, thanksgiving and intercession. Children who pray only for themselves and for things have not been taught how to pray. The Intergenerational Cell Group is an ideal place for children to learn how to pray.

Children do get bored if adults pray too long. Often adults wander on aimlessly in prayer thinking of things to say. Children tend to be direct and short in their praying. They don't wrap it up in flowery words. Some adults like to hear the flow of their own spiritual language.

Children's prayer can challenge adults to pray. An adult may feel too tongue-tied to pray in public but when they hear the simplicity of a child's prayer, they feel encouraged to try. Long sophisticated prayers from other adults do not help them to break the 'sound barrier'.

Often children will begin to pray for a clear need. They will pray for healing or comfort for someone. Later they learn to talk to God freely on any subject, as a friend talks with a friend.

Praying in the Spirit

Teach children how to pray in the Spirit. Before we ask God to do something, we should be asking the Holy Spirit to reveal to us what God wants to do in the situation (Romans 8:26–27). If our prayer is in tune with what God wants to do, we can expect that He will answer.

If the cell group practices praying in tongues, the children may very well do it too. Help them to understand what a prayer language is and how it should be used. Sometimes children break into a prayer language spontaneously if they are deeply moved by the Holy Spirit. It releases them from the tyranny of words.

Prayer Ideas for Adults and Children

1. Worship Prayer

When we worship the Lord, we speak to him out of love and thankfulness. Sometimes we can use a song or a psalm to express how we feel. We can imagine Jesus standing among us and imagine what we might want to say to Him. We can think up words to describe Him – perhaps words which begin with the same letter as our name. We can find pictures which remind us of the great things He has done. Some old magazines can supply some good pictures. We can take an object (like an orange) and think how it reminds us of God. We can use the Lord's Prayer as a model and express it in our own words.

2. Praying for Each Other

A child can pair up with an adult and learn to pray for cell group members. They could write the person's name on one side of a card and the prayer need on the other side. They could be that person's prayer partner for a week.

Every person could write a prayer need on a slip of paper and place it in a container. Then each person, adult and child, would draw out a prayer need and pray over it. Make sure the language is easy for a child to read.

Bring a large clock and set the hands to different times of the day. Each time ask someone what they were doing at that hour and pray for them in that situation. Give everyone a turn.

3. Special Occasions Prayer

When a special event happens in the cell group there should be some prayer to celebrate the event. A birthday prayer could take the letters of the person's name and the cell group could think up a blessing for each letter. Or the cell group could make up a prayer in which every sentence follows the letters of a word, like PENTECOST, or THANKSGIVING.

When a baby is born, the cell group could form a circle round the baby and start a chain of prayer in which each person adds a word or two of blessing. At Christmas, the cell group could make a Christmas present for Jesus in which they express their love and offering to him. Or, you could write a prayer on a card with key words left out and then ask the cell group adults and children to fill in the missing words.

4. Warfare Prayer

The cell group ought also to be praying strategically for the church, for the nation and for the world. Children can be powerful in their praying and strongholds in the world can be broken.

For this kind of praying, you need a newspaper or a television newsclip and a map. The group could pray for disaster areas, for missionaries, for world leaders, for leaders of their own country, for public issues. They should especially remember children in other parts of the world and pray about their pain and suffering.

Never think that children are not interested in what goes on in the world. They get really concerned when someone tells them what is happening.

They should also be praying for themselves and the cell group, to protect them from the attacks of Satan. They know they have an Enemy. They should be prepared to meet his attacks. They need to cover their cell group with prayer. Children need to know that prayer is not just a religious exercise, but it is also their powerful weapon in the struggle against evil. They should also be praying for their friends who do not know Jesus.

5. Covering Prayer

The children in the cell group need constant protection against the pressures of this world. As cell group members learn to love the children, they will want to pray for them. Some people may feel that is all they can do. Their prayers can affect the children and the church for years to come.

As you bless the children week by week, you are letting them know they are not alone in the world. Pray for the children's future, for their ministry and service, for their purity and courage. If the children are troublesome, pray for them. If you are tempted to give up on the children, pray for them. The outcome of this battle is too important for us to relax our guard.

*C*HILDREN IN CELL GROUP EVANGELISM

Does a child have an "oikos"?
What if a child from an unchurched family is converted?
Can children be involved in cell group outreach?
Can we reach children who have no church connection?

The Intergenerational Cell Group can be a powerful influence in the evangelism of children and their families. The cell group has the potential, not only to reach children and families, but also to provide them with a secure place where they can be nurtured in the body of Christ.

A cell group can reach out through the children in many ways. The most important evangelism happens when the children observe the lives of the adult cell group members, and decide they want to be like them. The cell group is a great place for children to discover Jesus for themselves.

Exploring the "oikos" of a Child
Even if the children themselves are already Christians, they do have an *oikos* (household) which includes family members, friends, tutors, teachers, classmates and team-members. Any of these may be reachable through the child. The cell group should explore the child's *oikos* to discover who might be responsive. They should help the children bring their friends to social or outreach events.

When a child brings a friend to his cell group, the adult members will need to help make him feel welcome. They should also visit his parents to begin to build a bridge of friendship. Parents and families need to know what kind of people are caring for their children. They will want to know that their children will get home safely. One family can "adopt" the child into their family while he is in the cell group.

A Child Winning Another Child
Children can learn how to share their faith. They can practice sharing John 3:16 with their friends and the cell group will pray for them as they try. Children are not afraid to tell others about Jesus if they have an easy method and they know

that other people are praying for them. Children should learn to pray for their friends and to be alert to outreach opportunities.

When the Child Has Unchurched Parents

When a child of non-Christian parents becomes a Christian, it is usually a shock to his/her parents and family. They are nearly always afraid that their children are being hooked into a cult. It is very threatening to find that their child has accepted a faith which may challenge some of their lifestyle and family values. Most parents suspect the enthusiasm will be short-lived, so they tolerate it for a while. They usually react very strongly against baptism.

The parents need to meet some adults from the cell group so that they see that Christians are normal people. Often their fears are based on hearsay and ignorance of the Christian faith. Also adults may be able to explain more clearly what has happened to their child. Children often do not have the words to tell their parents about their faith decision.

I would tend to say to parents something like this: *"Your son, James, has been with us a little while and he is a fine child. We have been learning more about Jesus and now he loves Jesus so much that he wants to follow Him. I know you would be proud of James if he turns out to be like Jesus. As a responsible parent, you will be wondering what this is all about. Perhaps you do not know too much about the Christian faith. If you would like to know more, we have a small group of people who are also asking questions about the Christian faith. You would be welcome to come along. There is no obligation. It is just a time when you can talk and find out some things you want to know."*

Sometimes parents will say, "Well if it makes some improvement in my son or daughter, it will be a good thing." This indicates they will be watching. If a child's new faith in Christ does produce some better attitudes and behavior, the parents are usually impressed. We need to help the children live daily in the presence and power of the Holy Spirit and trust Him to make the necessary changes. Don't let the children get too discouraged if they make mistakes and fail now and again. All Christians do that. Let parents see that the children know how to say 'sorry' and try harder next time.

Winning the Parents

The cell group should try to meet the unchurched parents socially at times. It may start with a shared meal. They may meet cell group members at a social event. Gradually the parents will come to feel more comfortable with these Christians and they will accept invitations to come to special occasions.

If there is a crisis in the family, they will be surprised to find members of the cell group ready to help. One person may provide a family meal or some transport during an emergency. Another person may baby-sit. If the family is moving house or renovating, they may appreciate some practical help. These gestures seem amazing to people in the community. Often they are not accustomed to people who are willing to help out of sheer love and concern.

As they get to know the members of the cell group, they will find people with similar interests. The cell group members will meet them socially. Maybe they support the same ball team, or they are both fanatic about plants. All the time the cell group is praying.

When the cell group is doing something together, the unchurched parents can be invited to help. They might prepare food or provide transport. In one church where the children were presenting a musical, some unchurched parents helped with stage management and making costumes. In time, some parents will like the Christians so much they will say, "I wish I could be like you people." At that point, it may be possible to lead them to accept Jesus.

Problems and Difficulties

Does this plan sound idealistic? Well, that's how it does work in some situations. When it doesn't, there are several reasons. The non-Christian parent may be suffering from too much pain and hostility from the past. They may have had a bad experience with Christians before. For such situations, it will take much more time and patience to build bridges of friendship.

Sometimes the cell group is not consistent enough. Cultivating friendship with the non-Christian parents of children is time-consuming and inconvenient. Sometimes the sacrifices seem too great. Or perhaps the Holy Spirit is not working in that person's life yet. We cannot win anybody by ourselves. If God is not working, then there is very little we can do. When we try to force the issue before he is ready, we may only damage people. Sometimes all we can do is to hold and encourage the child until the day comes when the family is united in Christ.

Children Joining Adults in Evangelism

When the cell group is planning some evangelistic activity, the children should be included in the plan. If the cell group invites an unchurched family to a special event, the children should be encouraged to act as hosts to the children of the family and to make them feel welcome. They should also come prepared with an activity which the new children will enjoy. If parents come to accept Jesus and their children do not yet know Him, the children of the cell group will need to be specially sensitive to the new children. They may be able to explain to the children better than the adults can.

If the cell group plans to have an interest group, there are ways the children can help. For instance, if the cell group plans to have a vacation program in a neighborhood, the children can make excellent junior helpers. If the cell group goes out to contact people in the community, they can go as part of the team. Children are very sensitive to people's feelings and they can help to pray for people.

If a cell group does some practical service for someone, the children can help with the project – whether it is painting, or tidying the yard, or cutting the grass. People are amazed to see children who are willing to help others.

Outreach Cell Groups or Clubs

Sometimes a cell group church will also have special outreach activities to reach children who are right outside the orbit of the church. Often these will be organized by specialist people who are called to this evangelistic ministry. The problem in the past has often been that the children were never incorporated into the life of the church. An Intergenerational Cell Group can be a link between the outreach cell group and the church.

If there is an outreach cell group or club in the same neighborhood, the Intergenerational Cell Group can decide to act as sponsors for that group. They can visit the club activities and get to know the children. They can get to know the parents of the children by joining some of the social activities. As the cell group gets to know the families of the unchurched homes, they become friends. When the Intergenerational Cell Group is having a special event, they can invite the parents of the club's children. When the family eventually accepts Christ, they will have a cell group ready to welcome them into the fellowship of the church. This could be a kind of interest group for the Intergenerational Cell Group and the children can be involved alongside their parents.

God can use the Intergenerational Cell Group to touch the lives of other people. Even children can win other people to Christ if they are given the opportunity. When children and their families are mobilized to reach out to others, the children begin to grow in their own faith and in their desire to win others for Christ. Evangelism in the Intergenerational Cell Group may be a powerful influence in developing the lives of the children.

A father was telling me about his Intergenerational Cell Group. One of the adults had brought along a non-Christian friend and all the adults were trying hard not to offend the man by being too religious. The nine-year-old girl was not so inhibited. She sat alongside the newcomer and said, "Sir, are you a Christian?"
"No, little girl, I guess I'm not," he replied.
"Would you like to be a Christian?" she asked.
"Well, I suppose I would," he said noncommitally.
"I can show you how," she said. And then and there, she led that man to Jesus in front of the whole cell group. He is now a Cell Group Leader.

$\mathcal{P}$ASTORING CHILDREN IN AN INTERGENERATIONAL CELL GROUP

Can the cell group handle the pastoral needs of the children?
How does the Cell Group Leader pastor the children?
Are there any guidelines to help us?

Somebody wins the trust of the child.

When you were a child, were there times when you would have loved to talk with someone you could trust? Most children have these moments and most parents want to believe that their children will always come to them. Sometimes, however, parents cannot counsel their own children.

There are all kinds of reasons for this. Sometimes the parents are too emotionally involved and the children fear they will over-react. Sometimes the parents *are* the problem and the children are too frightened to talk to them. This can happen in a marriage conflict or where sexual abuse is taking place. Sometimes children feel ashamed that they are not living up to their parents' expectations.

Pastoring Children in the Cell Group

The Intergenerational Cell Group is a place where children come under the covering of a small community. Other Christian adults will be interacting with the children in the cell group. Sometimes observers can see more than parents who live too close to the situation.

In the cell group, there may be someone who wins the trust of the child. This should not be a threat to the parents. Parents often need an ally, a friend who can give help in time of trouble.

A cell group can minister to a child through prayer. When children are brave enough to share a problem with the cell group, or in the Kids' Slot, they need to know that the group believes that God can do something about it. They may be helped through a Bible verse or a word from the Lord directed specially to them. When the cell group prays for the child, he/she feels a sense of belonging to a group who cares.

The Role of the Cell Group Leader

The leader of the cell group has overall responsibility for pastoring the people in the group. However, the leader does not have to do it all. He/she may feel rather inadequate to pastor children. If the child needs help, he/she would probably need to speak to the child's parents. They have the first responsibility over the child.

The Children's Coordinator or one of the other helpers may be able to speak personally to the child. If the problem is a fairly small one, it may be helped by the support and prayer of the whole cell group.

If the problem is serious, however, the Cell Group Leader may want to call in the help of the Zone Supervisor or Zone Pastor. It is seldom that a child's problem affects the child alone. More often, the whole family needs pastoral care. Such pastoral care can be given more easily in an Intergenerational Cell Group. If the problem is beyond the capability of the cell group, it may be necessary to call in professional help.

Guidelines for Action

1. Do not talk to children about their intense personal problems in front of other children. They will not talk freely and they will feel shame in front of their friends. If the problems begin to touch intimate matters of family life, where the parents need to be involved, the leader should arrange to meet the child at another time with the parent's permission. Often the parents will want to be there but sometimes the parents may need to trust the leader to talk with the child separately at first and then bring the family together. Sometimes, the presence of parents will silence the child.

2. Minor problems can be dealt with in the group and, sometimes, there may be other children involved. Often all the children will benefit by listening to the advice given by the cell group.

3. Listen to the child with full attention. Do not try to belittle the child's pain. Something that seems small to you can be very large to them and they feel the pain deeply.

4. Help them to understand what is happening. Often they only need an explanation of what is going on. Nobody bothers to explain to them and so they worry.

5. Pray with them to express God's power in the situation.

6. Help them to find out what God says to them through the Bible.

7. Help them to plan some small action they can do to help the situation. Part of their frustration arises out of their helplessness.

8. The child may need your help through the next few days or weeks, so keep in touch.

9. Do not try to handle problems which are beyond your skills. Report to your Zone Supervisor or Zone Pastor or IGC Facilitator.

10. Never talk with a child in a private place. Make sure that you have someone else within sight or sound.

What children need more than anything is to know that they are loved and accepted, first by God and then by the community around them. They need to be able to find forgiveness, to be freed from false guilt, to gain confidence for the future and to know that God will never let them down. They're not so different from us after all!

Ethical Standards

It is important that everyone in the church and in the cell groups should be aware of the ethical standards which the church has adopted. The public media are quick to report stories about children who, they suspect, have been exploited under the care of the church. We must maintain a standard of total transparency on this issue.

The Intergenerational Cell Group is probably the safest context for the care of children. The parents are present and the children are not shut away alone with an adult. The cell group surrounds the children and the group is likely to sense any unhealthy attitudes in any disturbed adult.

Our cell groups must protect the children. It is not just that the law demands it. God demands it. Jesus pronounces judgement on any person who causes one of his little ones to stumble.

On the other hand, we should also protect each other from false accusations. Our society is reaching the point where any affection shown towards children is suspect. We need to be able to give our children love and affirmation in a safe context.

ℬAPTISM AND THE LORD'S SUPPER IN AN INTERGENERATIONAL CELL GROUP

Suppose a child in the cell group wants to be baptized?
What does the Cell Group Leader do?
What if a child from a non-Christian home wants baptism?
May children in the cell group celebrate the Lord's Supper?

In an Intergenerational Cell Group the children are likely to see cell members being baptized and taking the Lord's Supper. It is part of cell group life. As children witness people in the cell group being baptized, they will ask when they too can be baptized to show that they follow Jesus. They will also want to share the Lord's Supper if they have accepted Jesus as their Lord and Savior.

The request may come from the child directly or from the child through his/her parents. If the cell group has known the child for some time, they will have a good idea of the level of the child's spiritual understanding. The cell group will help the parents either to support the request or to comfort the child if the group decides that it is not yet the right time.

The group should be very open to the Spirit of God through prayer and discernment to make the right decision. It is a family decision. If the parents, the Cell Group Leader and the cell group agree that God is calling the child into witnessing his/her faith in baptism, this would be a good procedure:

1. The Cell Group Leader and/or the Zone Pastor should talk to both parents to hear how the request for baptism was made and why the parents support the request.

2. The Cell Group Leader would talk to the child's Sunday leaders to find out more about his spiritual experience.

3. A Zone Pastor or Children's Pastor should talk with the child, asking that he/she explains how he/she received Jesus and why he/she wants to be baptized. The child should be encouraged to share this with the cell group also.

4. This process should not be hurried. If the Holy Spirit is moving in the life of a child, He will stir up a persistent desire which will not fade away.

5. The child should witness at least one baptismal service before he/she is baptized.

6. If the child's baptism is approved, it should be a significant celebration in which the family and the cell group members all participate. We want to create a strong spiritual memory.

7. Someone in the child's natural or spiritual family should undertake to be a special prayer partner with the child.

What if the Child Comes from a Non-Christian Home?

If the cell group knows that the child is a true believer and is being called by the Holy Spirit to be baptized, the child's sponsor and/or the Cell Group Leader should visit the parents and explain what baptism means. If they give permission for the child to be baptized, the same procedure should be followed.

If the parents refuse permission for their child to be baptized, the group should accept that decision. We should not encourage children to openly rebel against their parents. We might ask the parents if there would be a time when they might allow their child to make his/her own choice. The cell group then has the role of praying with the child and helping him/her to bear the disappointment. They could also pray for the salvation of the parents.

Should Children Receive the Lord's Supper?

In one church three eight-year-old girls waited to speak with the pastor. "Pastor," they said, "when you were talking to the people before the Lord's Supper, you said that anyone who truly loves Jesus is free to take part. We love Jesus, so why can't we take part?"

Hedging for time the pastor said he would talk to his elders about it. It was discussed seriously and a few weeks later they held the first Lord's Supper which included children. Parents were given the responsibility of deciding whether their child should partake of the Lord's Supper. The pastor explained what the

Lord's Supper means. Some fathers served their own children, as family priests. I overheard one little girl say to her sister, "You don't just take it because you're hungry. You take it because you love Jesus."

The Lord's Supper in a Cell Group

The cell group is a natural place to celebrate the Lord's Supper. It first began in a small group of Jesus' intimate friends. It is a family affair. In the early church, whole households gathered to remember the Lord together.

Fathers and mothers can serve their own children as they come to faith. They know the sincerity of the child's decision. They can also explain what the symbols mean. Very small children may genuinely love Jesus but have very little idea of what the symbols mean. They can be included by giving them a special blessing. One small group gave the children a grape as a token for the future.

Once children can perceive the meaning of the symbols, there is no real reason why they should not participate. Sharing at the Lord's table does not depend on age or maturity. Children who come to the Lord's table should understand, as all of us must, that partaking of the symbols of Christ's death is a serious matter. It should be done with reverence. Many children have a sense of holy awe at the Lord's table and they feel the presence of the Lord in a special way.

Sometimes children like to prepare a song or a special act of worship for the Lord's Supper. They may want to read a special Scripture passage. They should be encouraged to participate where they can. Even cleaning up the cups is an act of service they can share in.

If there are children who are not yet ready for the Lord's Supper, the parents should explain to the child why some children have been invited to participate. Each child will be invited when the right time comes. God will tell them when it is the right time.

When children share in the Lord's Supper, they feel that they are a part of the family of God. They focus on what Jesus has done for them and they pledge their allegiance to Him all over again. It is a precious moment for both children and parents.

*W*HAT HAPPENS ON SUNDAYS?

Is this the end of Children's Ministry on Sundays?
Should the children come into adult worship?
How can adult worship be meaningful to the children?
What should a Children's Church be like?

If the principal responsibility for nurturing the children of the church belongs to the family within the context of the Intergenerational Cell Group, what happens to the children on Sundays?

If we follow the pattern of the adult cell group, the children should meet on Sunday for **worship, celebration, teaching and ministry**. This can happen in two contexts.

1. The children can be part of the adult worship for all or part of the time.
If the children are part of the adult service, the leaders are responsible for making the service welcoming and friendly to the children. Children should not be bored to death by being spectators in the adult worship. Neither should adults have to tolerate "kiddy" worship. Both children and adults should be able to worship intergenerationally. This means involving the children at all levels – not as "items" but as part of the normal worship routine.

Children can sing, dance, play instruments, pray, read the Bible, share with families and participate in sermon-related activities. Some churches prefer to have the children leave the service before the message. Other churches have the children over a certain age sit right though the whole service. This depends to some extent on the ability of the pastor to communicate with both children and adults. The children can also respond to the message and receive ministry.

2. The children can have their own Children's Church.
In a Children's Church, the children have the same kind of experience as the adults do in their church service. They worship and praise with similar enthusiasm and style. They pray and receive words from the Lord. They

receive teaching, usually from a skilled children's teacher/preacher. They can respond to the message through small groups or through an invitation. The message can be presented by using any creative method, such as drama, visuals, games or object lessons.

Often the older children will take leadership and help with worship activities, with prayer and with ministry to younger children. They can also do practical tasks like managing the overhead projector transparencies. Children love to help and they take their responsibilities seriously. There is far less bad behavior when the children are equipped to serve other children.

The Children's Church is not just another version of Sunday School. When it is possible, the message for the children can follow the same theme as the message for the adults, so that the whole family can discuss it when they get home. The message which is preached on Sunday will become the core of the discussion at the Intergenerational Cell Group during the week. The Sunday worship and the Intergenerational Cell should be working together with the parents to help them unite all the child's spiritual teaching. Family worship can also become part of the teaching cycle.

There are some strong reasons for the children and the adults to worship together. Children enrich the service, bringing a freshness into it. They see the adults worshiping and they model their worship on what they see. If church is too boring for children, it is also too boring for adults.

However, children are not bored when they see God at work. It is never boring to see the Holy Spirit in action changing people's lives. When children feel the presence of the Lord, they are filled with awe and wonder. They need to know of the power of God, first-hand through seeing it, not second-hand through hearing about it.

If we want our children to become strong second-generation Christians, we should allow them to come as close as possible to the powerful action of God. We will not separate them from the adults. We will enable parents to fulfil the role God has given them by giving them a place where they find support and help. The cell group church has a place for children within their own families and near to the heart of God.

*A*PPENDIX A

Code of Ethics for Children's Leaders

Believing that God is calling me to serve children...

1. My first priority in leading children will be to help them grow according to their abilities in all areas of life: physically, socially, academically, emotionally and spiritually.

2. I will meet with the children's families so that we can get to know and understand one another, for the benefit of the children. I will also try to understand and respect the children's cultural backgrounds.

3. I will give the parents or care-givers full information about the program I am leading and what time it begins and ends. I will cooperate with them in seeing that the children get home safely.

4. I will not do anything to undermine a child's trust. I will try to protect the children from all forms of abuse while they are in my care.

5. If I suspect that children may be suffering from the abusive actions of another person, I will report that suspicion to a responsible leader.

6. If I wish to talk with children alone, it will be within the sight and sound of other people.

7. I will answer the children's questions openly and honestly. I will keep the parents informed on how their children are responding in their attitudes and behavior and in their growth in maturity and faith.

8. I will work with the children to set some agreed guidelines for acceptable behavior within the group. I will expect the children to act on the basis of these guidelines and if a child consistently breaks them, I will try to find out why.

9. If a child is distressed, I will try to offer comfort. I will help the child find the appropriate help for his/her needs. I will pray for each child regularly.

$\mathscr{A}$PPENDIX B

How to Lead a Child to Christ

I would like to introduce the booklet, **"Breaking the Barrier"**. This is a presentation of John 3:16, as shown on page 125. This explains God's plan of salvation through a story, with the use of stickers which the child can place on a diagram in the centre page of the booklet. When the diagram is completed, the way of salvation is very clear.

1. The booklet begins with the idea of God's love for us and His desire that we should be with Him forever.

2. Our sin creates a barrier between us and God. The barrier is called Sin. Sin means living without God and choosing to be bad. Sin always leads to death.

3. People try many different ways to break the barrier and get back to God. They try to be good. They may worship other gods. They may try being kind. They may even go to church. We cannot break the sin barrier by ourselves.

4. God loves us so much that He sent His Son Jesus to die for us. (At this point, one half of the cross shows His descent into the world.) People hated him so much they killed him on a cross. (Complete the cross shape.) Jesus came alive and broke the Sin Barrier.

5. Now we can come to the cross of Jesus. If we accept His death for us and ask Him to forgive our sin we can go back to God by breaking the Sin Barrier through the cross. The only other way leads to death.

6. The children are then encouraged to ask God to forgive their sins and to come back to God. They are asked to read John 3:16 putting their own name in the appropriate spaces.

The advantage of this booklet is that it is so easy to read and is so attractive that the children will feel happy to share it again with their friends and family. It is designed for children to use with other children.

Make sure the child is discipled by someone in the cell group.

WHAT HAPPENED WHEN YOU BECAME A CHRISTIAN

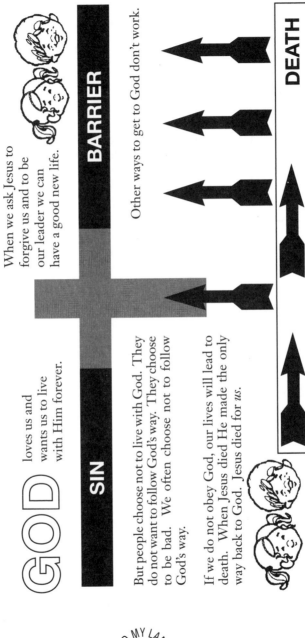

GOD loves us and wants us to live with Him forever.

SIN

But people choose not to live with God. They do not want to follow God's way. They choose to be bad. We often choose not to follow God's way.

If we do not obey God, our lives will lead to death. When Jesus died He made the only way back to God. Jesus died for *us*.

When we ask Jesus to forgive us and to be our leader we can have a good new life.

BARRIER

Other ways to get to God don't work.

DEATH

Talk about this diagram with your parents or sponsor.

FEED MY LAMBS
page
125

✍APPENDIX C

Worship Songs for Intergenerational Cell Groups

Number	Song	Key
A 001	A New Commandment	D
A 002	Abba Father (When children speak...)	D
A 003	Ah, lalala lala le lu jah (Take another hand)	D
A 004	Ah Lord God, Thou Hast Made the Heavens	D
A 005	Amazing Grace	E
A 006	Amen, Praise the Lord	D
A 007	As David Did...	Dm
A 008	As the Deer Pants for the Water...	D
A 009	As We Gather May Your Spirit	D
A 010	Awesome God (Our God is an awesome God)	C
B 001	Be Bold! Be Strong!	A
B 002	Be Ye Kind to One Another	C
B 003	Beautiful, Beautiful, Jesus Is Beautiful	C
B 004	Because He Lives	G
B 005	Behold What Manner of Love	D
B 006	Bind Us Together	D
B 007	Binding the Strong Man	D
B 008	Bless the Lord, O My Soul	G
B 009	Born Again, Born to Win	Gm
B 010	Bring a Psalm to the Lord	Fm
C 001	Celebrate (Come on and celebrate..)	D
C 002	Celebrate Jesus, Celebrate	F
C 003	Change My Heart, O God	C
C 004	Clap Your Hands and Sing to the Lord	D
C 005	Clap Your Hands All You People	E
C 006	Come, Bless the Lord	E
C 007	Come Holy Spirit, Fall Afresh on Me....	D
C 008	Come Let Us Offer the Sacrifice	E
C 009	Come Let Us Worship and Bow Down	D
E 001	Emmanuel	C
E 002	Everybody Ought to Know	C

Number	Song	Key
E 003	Exalt the Lord Our God	D
F 001	Fear Not, for I Am with You	Em
F 002	Forever Friends (All round us things are changing)	D
F 003	Forever Grateful (I'm forever grateful to you…)	D
F 004	For the Lord Is Marching On	Cm
F 005	From the Rising of the Sun	E
G 001	Give Thanks with a Grateful Heart	G
G 002	Give Thanks to the Lord for He is Good…	D
G 003	God Can Do Anything, Anything…	D
G 004	God Answers Prayer (Have you ever talked to God above..)	G
G 005	God Is Great, God is Good…	D
G 006	God Is Love, Open Up Your Heart	D
G 007	God Is Our Father and We Are All His Children	D
G 008	God Is So Good	D
G 009	God Will Make a Way	D
G 010	God's Love, Sweet and Wonderful	D
G 011	God's Not Dead	D
G 012	Great and Mighty Is the Lord	E
G 013	Great and Mighty Army (There's a great and mighty army)	D
H 001	Hail Jesus, You're My King	C
H 002	He Is Lovely, He is Holy	D
H 003	He Is My Everything	D
H 004	He Is the King of Kings	D
H 005	He's Able	D
H 006	He's the Children's Savior (I know someone)	F
H 007	He's the Lord of the Sunshine	D
H 008	Heaven Is a Wonderful Place	C
H 009	Heaven Is in My Heart (Oh -O-O-O-O)	D
H 010	Heavenly Father, I Appreciate You	E
H 011	Here We Are, Gathered Together as a Family	D
H 012	His Banner Over Me Is Love	D
H 013	His Love Is Warmer than the Warmest Sunshine	C
H 014	Holiness Unto the Lord	G
H 015	Holy Ground	F
H 016	Holy Lamb of God	D
H 017	Hosanna, Hosanna in the Highest	G
H 018	How Excellent Your Name Is	E

Number	Song	Key
I 001	I Am a Christian (I am a C-H-R-I-S-T-I-A-N)	D
I 002	I Am So Glad that Jesus	D
I 003	I Have Decided to Follow Jesus	C
I 004	I Just Want to Praise You	E
I 005	I Love to Praise Him	D
I 006	I Love You, Lord…	G
I 007	I Love You, Jesus	D
I 008	I Sing Praises to Your Name	G
I 009	I Stand in Awe of You	A
I 010	I Surrender All	D
I 011	I Want to Let Jesus Love Me	D
I 012	I Will Arise and Go Forth	D
I 013	I Will Celebrate His Name (I will lift my voice)	Dm
I 014	I Will Celebrate, Sing unto the Lord	Dm
I 015	I Will Enter His Gates	D
I 016	I Will Love Thee	Dm
I 017	I Will Praise You, Lord	D
I 018	I Will Put on My Robe of Righteousness	Bb
I 019	I Will Rejoice, I Will Rejoice	D
I 020	I Will Sing, I Will Sing a Song unto the Lord	D
I 021	I Will Worship You Lord, with All of My Heart	Dm
I 022	I Worship You, Almighty God…	G
I 023	I'll Sing of the Mercies of the Lord Forever	C
I 024	I've Got a Home in Gloryland	D
I 025	I've Got Peace Like a River	C
I 026	If You Want to Be Great (Servant of All)	Eb
I 027	In Him We Live and Move…	D
I 028	In His Time, In His Time	C
I 029	In Moments Like These	D
I 030	In My Life, Lord, Be Glorified	D
I 031	In the Name of Jesus	E
I 032	In the Presence of Your People	Dm
I 033	Into My Heart	D
I 034	It is You, It is You…	D
I 035	It's a Great Day to Praise the Lord	D
I 036	It's a Happy Day	F
I 037	It's No Longer I that Liveth	G

Number	Song	Key
J 001	Jehovah Jireh	Fm
J 002	Jesus Christ is the Lord of All	D
J 003	Jesus, I Love You, I Bow Down Before You	C
J 004	Jesus Loves Me	D
J 005	Jesus Loves the Little Children	D
J 006	Jesus, Name Above All Names	D
J 007	Jesus, We Celebrate Your Victory	D
J 008	Jesus, We Enthrone You	G
J 009	Jesus, You're the Sweetest Name of All	D
J 010	John 3:16	F
J 011	Joy, Down in My Heart (Deep Deep Down)	D
J 012	Joy is the Flag	D
K 001	King of Kings and Lord of Lords	Em
L 001	Lead Me to the Cross of Jesus	D
L 002	Let All Creation and in the Heavenlies	G
L 003	Let God Arise	C
L 004	Let the Redeemed of the Lord Say So	C
L 005	Let There Be Love Shared Among Us	F
L 006	Let Us Adore the Ever Living God	Dm
L 007	Let Us Come Together, Praise the Name	F
L 008	Let Your Spirit Rise Within Me	G
L 009	Listening to Jesus, Listening Every Day	D
L 010	Little by Little, One Step at a Time	E
L 011	Lord, I Lift Your Name on High	G
L 012	Lord I Will, Lord, I Will.	G
L 013	Lord, We've Come to Worship You	D
L 014	Lord, You Are More Precious Than Silver	D
L 015	Love in Any Language	D
L 016	Love One Another for Love is of God.	D
L 017	Love the Lord Your God with All Your Heart	G
M 001	Majesty	Bb
M 002	Make a Joyful Noise unto the Lord All the Earth	C
M 003	Make Me a Servant, Humble and Meek	D
M 004	Mighty Is Our God	E
M 005	Mighty Warrior	E
M 006	More Than Anything	D
M 007	My Beloved is Mine and I am His	D

Number	Song	Key
M 008	My Glory and the Lifter of my Head	D
M 009	My Life is In You, Lord	G
O 001	O How He Loves You and Me	C
O 002	O-B-E-Y Obey Your Mum and Dad	D
O 003	Old Gospel Train (I'm travelling on the Hallelujah Line)	D
O 004	O Lord, You're Beautiful	F
O 005	One God (Hear O Israel the Lord thy God...)	Dm
O 006	One Voice (Father, we ask of You this day)	F
O 007	Only by Grace Can We Enter	D
O 008	Open Our Eyes, Lord	D
P 001	Pass It On (It only takes a spark...)	D
P 002	Pearly Shell	D
P 003	People of the Lord (There is one body...)	F
P 004	Praise Him Praise Him Jesus	D
P 005	Praise Him, Praise Him, Praise Him in the Morning	D
P 006	Praise Him, Praise Him with Our Song	F
P 007	Praise Ye the Lord (Hallelu, Hallelu...)	D
R 001	Rejoice in the Lord, Always	D
R 002	Revival in the Land	D
R 003	Rise and Shine	D
S 001	Say to the Lord, "I Love You" (Kids Praise 2)	D
S 002	See His Glory, See His glory	D
S 003	Seek Ye First the Kingdom of God	D
S 004	Shine, Jesus, Shine	A
S 005	Sing Hallelujah to the Lord	Dm
S 006	Sing unto the Lord a New Song	Dm
S 007	Something Beautiful, Something Good	E
S 008	Son of God, This is our Love Song	D
S 009	Spirit of the Living God	F
S 010	Stand Up and Shout It	G
S 011	Stand Up, Stand Up for Jesus	D
T 001	Thank you, Jesus for your love for me	D
T 002	Thank you, Thank you Jesus	D
T 003	The Blessing of the Lord Shall Be Upon His People	E
T 004	The God of Israel Is Mighty	E
T 005	The Greatest Thing in All My Life	E
T 006	The Joy of the Lord	D

Number	Song	Key
T 007	The Lord Reigns	D
T 008	The Steadfast Love of the Lord	D
T 009	The Sweetest Name of All (Jesus, you are the Sweetest Name)	C
T 010	The Way that He Loves	C
T 011	There's a River of Life	D
T 012	This Is the Day	D
T 013	This Little Light of Mine	D
T 014	Through Our God We Shall Do Valiantly	Cm
T 015	Thy Lovingkindness Is Better Than Life	D
T 016	To Be Like Jesus	D
T 017	To Keep Your Lovely Face	D
T 018	Touch Your Fingers	D
T 019	Trust and Obey	D
T 020	Turn Your Eyes upon Jesus	D
W 001	Walking with Jesus, Walking Every Day	E
W 002	We Are Heirs of the Father	E
W 003	We Are Here to Praise You	D
W 004	We Are One in the Bond of Love	C
W 005	We Believe in God the Father (Kendrick)	F# m
W 006	We Bring the Sacrifice of Praise	D
W 007	We Choose the Fear of the Lord	Em
W 008	We Have a Vision For This Nation	F
W 009	We Place You on the Highest Place	D
W 010	What a Good Good Lord We Have	D
W 011	What a Mighty God We Serve	D
W 012	When the Spirit of the Lord Is In This Place	Dm
W 013	With All My heart (With my lips I will bless You)	D
W 014	With All My Heart I Will Follow after You	D
W 015	With Christ in the Vessel	E
W 016	Worthy, You are Worthy, King of Kings	D
Y 001	You Are Crowned with Many Crowns	E
Y 002	You Are My Hiding Place	Am
Y 003	You Have Won the Victor's Crown	D
Y 004	Your Steadfast Love	F

(Compiled by Tan Din Lua)

$\mathscr{A}$PPENDIX D

Icebreakers

1. Word-forming (Relationships)
Organize the group into pairs. Let each pair write down as many words as they can think of, from the letters MACDONALDS (or choose your own word). No proper names or slang words are allowed. Suggested time limit: 5 minutes.

2. Coordinated Jump (Team building)
Form a circle. Everyone put their arms over the shoulders of the persons on their left and right. At the word, 'GO' everyone must jump (both feet off the ground) at the same instant. The ones who do not or are too fast or too slow, drop out of the circle. Repeat until only a few are left.

3. Who Am I? (Openness – specially good for use outdoors))
Each person finds something which tells something about themselves; their character, their likes and dislikes, their background, their job. Ask each member to show what they have selected and explain why. For example, I picked a rock because it is strong and smooth and old.

4. Introductions (Learning names)
At a signal, everyone must move around the room shaking hands with as many people and asking their names. Each person must remember as many names as possible. At the end of two minutes, they all sit down and the leader asks each person how many names they can remember.

5. World Trip (Sharing dreams)
The leader starts by saying: I'm going on my world trip from (my town) to (choice of destination). The next person in the circle says: On my world trip I'm going from (the leader's choice) to (this person's choice). Continue in this way round the circle. Get one person to write down the sequence of places. When it gets back to the leader again he says: On my world trip I'm coming home from (last choice) to (hometown). Then the writer reads out the journey you have all made.

6. World Views (Exploring value systems)
Bring old magazines and newspapers. Work in pairs to tear out five clippings which suggest the values that God is looking for in people. Then ask them to tear out five clippings of values that the world is looking for in people. Small children can do this but they need a partner. When they have finished, let the group compile what they have chosen.

7. Find Someone (Discovering one another)
Prepare slips of paper and provide pencils. Each member is to move round the room and find someone for each category.

1. ...plays the piano
2. ...plays golf
3. ...has two daughters
4. ...is left-handed
5. ...has freckles
6 ...with numbers 6 or 9 in their telephone number
7. ...goes to school
8. ...can name the twelve disciples of Jesus
9. ...watches cartoons at least twice a week
10....who does not drink coffee

8. Tick Tock (Building rapport)
The leader passes a colored block to person A on his left and says: This is a tick. The person says: A what? The leader replies: A tick.
Person A does the same thing to Person B on his left. Let this continue a few times till the pattern gets established. Then the leader starts a different block going in the opposite direction round the circle but this time he says: This is a tock. The person on the right replies: A what? Leader replies: A tock. Confusion is bound to set in. You could add more blocks if you choose.

9. Eliminations (Discovering one another)
Let everyone in the room stand up. Read out the following list slowly and ask people to sit down if they have done any of these things before, or it describes them.

1. *Squeeze toothpaste from the middle of the tube*
2. *Avoid big dogs*
3. *Have a friend or relative living in Australia*
4. *Eat hamburgers or potato crisps at least once a week*
5. *Have been caught for a traffic violation*
6. *Talk to plants*
7. *Regularly watch television after 11 pm*
8. *Read the newspaper at breakfast*
9. *On a diet*
10. *Drop your towel on the bathroom floor*
11. *Have been to Hawaii*
12. *Late to cell group this week*

If anyone is still standing at the end, give them a token prize for being the person in the room who has done absolutely nothing.

10. Word Associations (Relationships)
The leader suggests a word and the person on his left has to add a word which is associated with the word he has been given and this continues round the circle, e.g., Blue – sky – pilot – plane – mountain...
If the group cannot see the association, they need to ask the person who added the word. Keep going round the circle for some minutes. Small children may need help.

11. Getting to Know You (Relationships)
At any time you can use one or more of these questions as a getting-to-know-you exercise. Ask each person in the group to name:

1. *Their favorite food*
2. *Their favorite book of the Bible*
3. *Their favorite television program*
4. *Their favorite hobby*
5. *A country they would like to visit and why*
6. *An animal which they think is like them and why*
7. *A Bible event they would like to have witnessed*
8. *A person in the world they would like to meet*
9. *Their first idea of what they wanted to be in life*
10. *The thing they hate most*

12. Live Spelling (Relationships)
Give each person in the group cards which show one letter of the alphabet. It doesn't matter how many cards each person has but everyone should have some. When the leader calls out a word, the people have to put down the letters in the right order as quickly as possible. You could do this in teams if you wish.

13. Back to Back (Observation)
Ask two people to stand back to back. Do not warn them. Then ask each person:

1. What color shoes is your partner wearing?
2. What color eyes does your partner have?
3. Is your partner wearing a T-shirt?
4. What is the main color your partner is wearing?
5. Roughly how tall is your partner?
6. Is your partner wearing a ring?

You could add any other questions.
A variation of this icebreaker is to have two partners observe each other and then each person turns around and makes one small change to their appearance e.g., untie a shoe lace, unbutton a button. Then let their partner see if they can spot the difference.

14. Banana duel (Cooperation)
Put one adult and one child in each pair. Tie both left wrists together and give one partner a banana in their right hand. The aim is to peel the banana and feed them to their partner.

15. Balloon Person (Relationships)
Required: One round balloon and a felt pen.
Choose a person to blow up the balloon and tie it. He/she passes it to the next person who takes the felt pen to start drawing a face according to instructions. Ask the person to draw one ear, then pass it on. Next person draws, one eye and passes it on. Keep on adding features as each person

takes the balloon. You can include wrinkles or freckles, or teeth or anything else your imagination suggests. When everyone else has had a turn, the last person should give the balloon person a name. The leader then solemnly welcomes the balloon person to the group.

16. A Measured Minute (Building rapport)
Required: a cassette player and a stop watch
Put people in pairs. Tell them that you are all going to measure one minute. Play some music on a cassette player in the background. Start time. Each pair tries to guess when one minute is up. When the pair thinks the minute is up they say "Stop". The leader stops the stop watch and checks the time. He/she tells them how many seconds have elapsed and how many there are still to go. Start the stop watch again until another pair calls out. The winners are those who get closest to a full minute. No use of watches.

17. How Are You Feeling? (Openness)
Ask each person to draw a face expressing how they are feeling. They may write the word if they can't draw. Put all the pieces of paper in a container in the middle. Then each person draws out a piece of paper and reads it aloud. The person who draws the paper, or someone else in the group, can say a word of encouragement to the anonymous person.

18. Miles of Smiles (Relationships)
Ask each person in the group to smile and measure their smile with a tape measure. Total measurements up. Then ask each person to estimate the number of times they smile in a day. Again total up, then use a calculator to multiply the first total by the second. What is the distance covered?

19. Written on My Hand (Caring)
Provide pens and paper.
Ask each person to put one hand on a piece of paper and draw the outline of his/her hand on the paper. Take the outline of the hand and ask five people to write their names on each finger. During prayer time, each member prays for the people whose names are on his/her hand.

20. Fire Drill (Values)

Let the people imagine that the fire alarm has sounded and they have 30 seconds to rescue their most valuable possession. Let them write down their first choice (e.g. photos, love letters, exam notes, insurance policy, teddy bear). If they had time to get two, what would be their second choice? Let them explain their choices.

21. People to People (Mixer)

The group forms a circle, except the leader who stands in the center. The leader snaps his fingers and chants "people to people" and each member finds a partner. Whenever he wishes, he changes the chant to "hand to hand", or "feet to feet", or "toes to toes", or "elbows to elbows" etc. As the chant changes, the partners join hands to hands, or feet to feet, etc. At the call "people to people", everyone has to change partners. You can make it more challenging by calling two body parts e.g., "hand to foot".

22. Old Aunt Amy (Building rapport)

The purpose of this icebreaker is to guess whether Old Aunt Amy died last night. The leader will begin by saying: "Old Aunt Amy, she died last night, she died last night. Did she die?" Then he points to anyone in the group. They have to reply "Yes" or "No". The trick is when the leader says: "Listen carefully," before he says the phrase, the answer is "Yes." If he omits the catch phrase, the answer is "No". If the person answers wrongly he is out.

23. Scissors (Building rapport)

A pair of scissors is handed round the circle of people. As each person gives the scissors to the next person they say, "Crossed" or they may say "uncrossed." The person passing the scissors tends to focus attention on the scissors by crossing or uncrossing the blades. People who do not know the secret cannot easily get the right word because they think it relates to the scissors. Actually it relates to whether the givers have crossed or uncrossed their legs as they sit. Gradually people get the idea until everyone can get it right.

24. Spider Web (Relationships)

Divide into groups of six to eight and form circles. Instruct members of each group to extend their right hands across the circle and grasp the left hands of the other members who are approximately opposite them. Then have the people reach out their left hands and grasp the right hands of their opposites. The task is to unravel the spider web of interlocking arms without letting go of anyone's hands.

25. Birthday Order (Discovering one another)

Let everyone line up in the room according to their birth dates, starting from January and ending in December. Special celebration for people who have their birthdays in the current month. Special token prize for the person whose birthday is nearest to Christmas. You can also do this with the age or height of the members

26. Sharing

Group people in fours and give each person a small puzzle made of a square of paper or card cut into four pieces. Every person should have the same puzzle. Give everyone four pieces but not the right pieces to complete the puzzle. The aim is for each person to complete the puzzle as fast as they can each one for himself. When one person needs another piece they must ask someone else for the piece they want and it must be handed over even if they think they need it. They cannot demand it back immediately. Time how long it takes for all four to finish.

Then have another turn in which the aim is for everyone to complete their puzzles in the shortest possible time.

27. Tactile Copier

Let everyone line up in the room and give the last person a simple diagram (e.g., a house or a car). The last person draws the diagram on the back of the person in front of him, and that person draws it on the back of the person in front of him. When the diagram reaches the first person they need to say what they think was drawn on their back.

28. Stand Up (Cooperation)

Let two people sit on the floor back to back. They link both arms firmly. Then they try to stand up together. Let other pairs have a try. You can also ask people to stand with their heels and calves touching a wall and ask them to pick up a piece of paper

29. Trust Walk (Personal trust)

Pair the people up. Blindfold one partner and let the other take them on a conducted walk around the adjacent area. After a time, the other partner should be blindfolded. When they all come back, let them share how they felt entrusting themselves to another person.

30. Changing the World

Go round the group asking each person, "If you had the authority to do one thing to improve the world what would it be?" (Let's assume that the very best thing would be for everyone to come to know Jesus.) You can also ask: "If you could change one thing about yourself, what would it be?"

(Compiled by Aw Yew Lin)

$\mathscr{A}$PPENDIX E

KIDS' SLOT ACTIVITIES

1. Drama

It's very useful to have a box or dress-up clothes available.

A. Re-enacting Bible Events This could be unrehearsed. Children can make up amazing dialog if they are encouraged.

B. Role-playing Real Life Situations Role plays are useful for reinforcing the application and for demonstrating when memory verses can be used.

C. Praise and Worship Drama The children can interpret a praise psalm or song in dramatic mime and movement.

D. Acting to Express Feelings Give the children an action to do, such as, getting home from school. They can do the action in various moods, such as grumpiness, happiness, boredom.

E. Acting to Identify With Others Find a story in a newspaper or book and ask the children to act the way the people would feel, e.g., a family in famine.

F. Dramatic Readings Teach the children how to read Scripture as a dramatic event. They can learn to be a verse choir which can lead the worship in the cell group or elsewhere.

G. Video Drama If someone in the cell group has a video camera, they could film one of the children's plays so it can be shown elsewhere.

2. Art

A. Drawing and Painting Use a variety of media: felt-pens, chalks, pastels, paints, pencils.

B. Fingerpainting The children spread thick paint and paste on a piece of paper and make patterns with their fingers.

C. Seed and Bark Pictures Make a picture using seeds and small items like rice, lentils, grass-heads, bark, split peas, lichens.

D. Pasta Pictures Make a picture with pasta shapes and spray them with paint later. You should soften the spaghetti for outlines.

E. Murals Draw and paint one section of a story per week to cover the whole unit. Join them together to make a continuous story at the end.

F. Collages Use magazine pictures to create a whole new picture.

G. Mosaic Pictures Use torn up scraps of colored paper from magazines to fill in a simple design.

H. Comic Strip Draw a comic strip to tell your story. You can use stick figures.

I. Stained Glass Windows Splash color onto newsprint paper and overlay it with a black outline which gives the design. Younger children can do the color, while the older children cut out the design.

J. Fabric Painting The children can design their own theme T-shirts, sneakers, hats or scarves. The clothing does not need to be new. Fabric paints can refurbish old clothing.

K. Over-head Projector Transparencies Use permanent pens to create wonderful praise transparencies for use in cell group or public worship.

L. Maps and Plans Children love drawing maps. It could be maps of Biblical events, or maps of their community, which the group could use in prayer walks. They could draw maps of places in the world where the missionaries are living. They could even draw imaginary maps for stories. They also like to draw plans. They could draw plans of Noah's ark, or Solomon's temple or their own church.

M. Banners These can be praise banners or theme banners, or zone identification banners. Materials should be of durable materials, such as fabric, felt or vinyl.

3. Crafts

A. Paper cut-outs These can be figures to tell a story, folded paper dolls, or geometric designs like tangrams

B. Paper folding Origami

C. Hessian darning Use large tapestry needle and colored wool to decorate mats, bookmarks, etc. Simple darning or daisy stitches look great.

D. Sewing Cards Find a bold picture and make stitch points on it so that the children can sew the picture in colored wool.

E. Modelling Create a scene which tell your story using play dough or other modelling material. You can also ask children to create a shape which expresses how they feel. Other forms of modelling include cardboard cut-outs or a shoe-box scene.

F. Photography Polaroid cameras create an instant result for the children. They can keep a photo album of themselves. They can photograph special events or drama. They can photograph visitors to the cell group or people they can help. Or they can collect photos of things to thank God for.

G. Virtually any craft can be adapted for the use of children. There are excellent children's craft books in most libraries. Projects should not be too complicated. However it is good for the project to last more because the children like to come back to it.

4. Games

Almost any games can be adapted for use in the cell group. Party games can be adapted to express values and relationships. Dice or spinner games can be used for selecting prayer items or Bible verses. Some traditional board games can be adapted for our purposes. Examples:

Snakes and Ladders can illustrate the journey towards God. The snakes should be labelled with the wrong things that trap us. The ladders should be named after the fruit of the Spirit.

Ludo can be adapted for praying for our friends. Give each counter the name of a friend who does not know Jesus. Then try to bring each friend home to Jesus.

Dominoes is a game even little children can play. Each time they set down a number, they can think of things to thank God for: 2 eyes, 1 house, 3 brothers, etc.

5. Nature and Science

A. Saucer Gardens Use paper dishes to create a tiny card with plants and moss and shells and flowers.

B. Grow Some Seeds Bulbs and pot plants.

C. Make a collection Can be anything: leaves, rocks, flowers, shells or pictures of butterflies.

D. Demonstrate a Simple Science Experiment It could be watching ice turn to liquid and then to steam. This is a good illustration of the Trinity.

E. Go for a Nature Walk Observe what is happening in the natural world in your neighborhood. Talk about the way God cares for His creation.

6. Music

A. Composition Children can be encouraged to write their own songs, both the words and the music. They can do it onto a cassette first and then get someone to write down the notation.

B. Performance Children can create music items, either vocal or instrumental.

C. Theme Music Children can choose music which creates a mood and find verses of Scripture to go with it. Some color pictures would add to the effect.

D. Movement and Music Children love to dance or work out movement which interpret the music.

6. Construction

Children love building things Use your imagination to see what you can do with junk materials. The sky's the limit.